PYTHON 3
Pocket Primer

PYTHON 3
Pocket Primer

James R. Parker

MERCURY LEARNING AND INFORMATION
Dulles, Virginia
Boston, Massachusetts
New Delhi

Publisher: David Pallai

MERCURY LEARNING AND INFORMATION
22841 Quicksilver Drive
Dulles, VA 20166
info@merclearning.com
www.merclearning.com
(800) 232-0223

James R. Parker. *Python 3* Pocket Primer.
ISBN: 978-1-68392-086-1

The publisher recognizes and respects all marks used by companies, manufacturers, and developers as a means to distinguish their products. All brand names and product names mentioned in this book are trademarks or service marks of their respective companies. Any omission or misuse (of any kind) of service marks or trademarks, etc. is not an attempt to infringe on the property of others.

Library of Congress Control Number: 2017934664
17181932   Printed in the United States of America on acid-free paper.

Our titles are available for adoption, license, or bulk purchase by institutions, corporations, etc. For additional information, please contact the Customer Service Dept. at (800) 232-0223 (toll free). Digital versions of our titles are available at: www.authorcloudware.com and other e-vendors. *Companion files for this title may be requested at info@merclearning.com.*

CONTENTS

Chapter 3: Sequences: Strings, Tuples, and Lists   35

PREFACE

This book is an effort to give a programmer sufficient knowledge of Python 3 to be able to work on their own projects. It is based on a much longer book that was intended for beginning programmers, and so most of the introductory material and basic computer science has been removed.

What remains is, first, a lot of code. Programming is something that must be practiced, and this book provides a lot of examples that are intended to inspire the explanations of programming language structures that otherwise lack context. Many of the examples are games or portions of games. That's because most of the audience are game players of one kind or another and can understand the examples. The code that implements the game is motivated by that understanding, although there are always many different actual programs that can be written to solve any one problem.

The example code was compiled on a PC running Windows 10, using Python 3.4 and the *PyCharm* GUI. Working code was copied directly into the manuscript and so should always be functional, but however hard we try, sometimes errors creep in during production. Please let me know if you find one.

There are a couple of unique features of this short book. One is the chapter on PyGame, which allows a programmer to handle graphics, control mouse and keyboard interaction, and play sounds and videos. The large example for that chapter is a *Lunar Lander* game.

Another feature is the chapter on communication, which makes use of one of Python's best features: a collection of modules for sending and receiving Email, communicating between computers, and working with Twitter and Web pages.

The disc that accompanies this book contains all of the code examples as complete working programs (also available for downloading from the publisher). This means that there is no need to type them in so they can be executed and perhaps modified or expanded. The disc also contains all of the figures in the book at their original size. Some of these are used as data for the programs, so it's good to have them.

There is a large code base in both Python 2.7 and Python 3, and one must take care when installing and using any module that it is compatible with the version of Python that has been installed—the two are incompatible.

Python 2 vs. Python 3

Here are the critical differences between the two versions of Python.

division   In Python 2, dividing two integers results in an integer: 3/2=1. In Python 3, '/' is floating point division, so 3/2 is 1.5.

byte   Python 2 has no **byte** type.

xrange   Python 3 has no **xrange** function.

exception   Python 3 requires that when raising an exception, the exception argument must be enclosed in parentheses. For example:

```
raise IOError ("missing file")   # Py3
```

as opposed to

```
raise IOError, "missing_file"   # Py2
```

print   In Python 2, print is a statement, but in Python 3 it is a function.

There are other minor differences. Also, some of the features of Python 2 that were considered to be mistakes were repaired in Python 3 (e.g., rounding, parsing user input using **input**()).

J. Parker
March 2017

## CHAPTER 1

COMPUTERS AND PROGRAMMING

We are going to learn a language called *Python*. It was developed as a general-purpose programming language and is a good language for teaching because it makes a lot of things easy. Quite a few applications have been built using Python, such as the games *Eve Online* and *Civilization IV*, *BitTorrent*, and *Dropbox* to name only a few. It is a bit like a lot of other languages in use these days in terms of structure (syntax) but has some simplifying ideas that will be discussed in later chapters.

In order to use a programming language, there are some basic concepts and structures that need to be understood at a basic level, and if you already program in Java or C++ then you likely already know a lot of these. The book will teach you Python by example; coding examples will be introduced by stating a problem to be solved. The problems to be solved in this chapter include the game of *rock-paper-scissors*. These problems will be the motivation for learning more about either the Python language itself or about methods of solving problems. Any computer programs in this book will execute on a computer running any major operating system once the free Python language download has been installed.

Executing Python

Installing Python is not too difficult, and involves downloading the installer, running it, and perhaps configuring a few specific details. This process can be found in many places on the Internet, including *http://docs.python-guide.org/en/latest/starting/installation/*. Python works on nearly any system. Once installed there are a few variations that can be used with it, the simplest probably being the Python Graphical User Interface or GUI. If running Python on a Windows PC, look at the Start menu for Python and click; a link named "IDLE (Python GUI)" will be seen, as shown in Figure 1.1. Click on this and the user interface will open. Click the mouse in the GUI window so that you can start typing characters there.

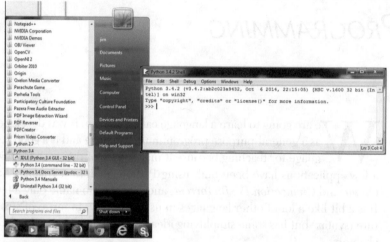

FIGURE 1.1. Running Python using IDLE.

Python can be run interactively in the GUI window. The characters ">>>" are called a *prompt*, and indicate that Python is waiting for something to be typed at the keyboard. Anything typed here will be presumed to be a Python program, or at least part of one. As a demonstration, type "1" and press "Enter." Python responds by printing "1." Why? When "1" was typed it was a Python expression, something to be evaluated. The value of "1" is simply "1," so that was the answer Python computed.

Now type "1+1." Python responds with "2." Python inputs what the user/ programmer types, evaluates it as a mathematical (in Python form) expression, and prints the answer. This is not really programming yet, because a basic two-dollar calculator can do this, but it is certainly a start.

IDLE is good for many things, but eventually a more sophisticated environment will be needed, one that can indent automatically, detect some kinds of errors, allow programs to be run and debugged and saved as *projects*. This kind of system is called an integrated development environment, or IDE. There are many of these available for Python, some costing quite a lot and some freely downloadable. The code in this book has been compiled and tested using one called *PyCharm*, but most IDEs out there would be fine, and it is largely a matter of personal preference. Basic *PyCharm* is free and it has a bigger brother that costs a small amount.

An advantage of an IDE is that it is easy to type in a whole program, run it, find the errors, fix them, and run it again. This process is repeated until the program works as desired. Multiple parts of a large program can be saved as separate files and collected together by the IDE, and they can be worked on individually and tested together. And a good IDE uses color to indicate syntax features that Python understands and can show some kinds of error while the code is being entered.

Rock-Paper-Scissors

Although this game is used by children to settle disputes and make random decisions such as "who goes first," it has been taken more seriously by adults. There are actually competitions where money is at stake. A televised contest in Las Vegas had a prize of $50,000. This game is not as trivial as it once was.

In this game each of two players selects one item from the list [rock, paper, scissors] in secret, and then both display their choice simultaneously. If both players selected the same item, then they try again. Otherwise, rock beats scissors, scissors beats paper, and paper beats rock. This contest can be repeated for a "best out of N" competition.

Both of these games form the first problem set, and serve as the motivation for learning the elements of the Python language.

Solving the *Rock-Paper-Scissors* Problem

The solution to this problem uses only basic language features. One solution to this problem is:

1) Select a random choice from the three items: rock, paper, or scissors. Save this choice in a variable named **choice**.
2) Ask the player for their choice. Use an integer value, where 1 = rock, 2 = paper, and 3 = scissors.
3) Read the player's selection into a variable named **player**.
4) If **player** is equal to **choice**:
5)   Print the message "Tie. We'll try again."
6)   Repeat from step 1.

7) If **player** is equal to rock:
8)   If **choice** is equal to scissors go to step 17
9)   Else go to step 18.
10) If **player** is equal to paper:
11)   If **choice** is equal to scissors go to step 17
12)   Else go to step 18.
13) If **player** is equal to scissors:
14)   If **choice** is equal to rock go to step 17
15)   Else go to step 18.
16) Print error message and terminate.
17) Print "computer wins" and terminate.
18) Print "You win" and terminate.

For each player selection, one of the alternate items will beat it and one will lose to it. Each choice is checked and the win/lose decision is made based on the known outcomes.

The solutions to both problems require similar language elements: a way to store a value (a *variable*), a way to execute specific parts of the program depending on the value of a variable or expression (an *if* statement), a way to read a value from the keyboard, a way to print a message on the screen, and a way to execute code repeatedly (a *loop*).

Variables and Values – Experimenting with the Graphical User Interface

A *variable* is a name that the programmer can define to represent some value, a number, or a text string generally. Not all strings or characters can be variable names. A variable cannot begin with a digit, for example, or with most non-alphabetic characters like "&" or "!," although in some cases beginning with "_" is acceptable. A variable name can contain upper- or lowercase letters, digits, and "_." Uppercase and lowercase are distinct, so the variables **Hello** and **hello** are different.

Programs often have variables named **i** or **x**. However, it is a good idea to select names that represent the kind of value that the variable is to contain, so as to communicate that meaning to another person, probably a programmer. For example, the value 3.1415926 should be stored in a variable named **pi**, because that's the name everyone else gives to this value.

In the GUI, type **pi = 3.1415926**. Python responds with a prompt, which indicates that it is content with this statement, and that it has no value to print. If you now type **pi**, the response will be **3.1415926**; the variable named **pi** that was just created now has a value.

In the syntax of Python, the name **pi** is a variable, the number **3.1415926** is a constant but also an *expression*, and the symbol **=** means *assign to*. In the precise domain of computer language, **pi = 3.1415926** is an *assignment statement* and gives the variable named **pi** the specified value.

Continuing with this example, define a new variable named **radius** to be 10.0 using an assignment statement **radius = 10.0**. If you type **radius** and press "enter," Python responds with **10.0**. Finally, we know that the circumference of a circle is **2πr** in math terms, or *2 times pi times the radius* in English. Type **2*pi*radius** into the Python GUI, and it responds with **62.831852**, which is the correct answer. Now type **circumference = 2*pi*radius**, and Python assigns the value of the computation to the variable **circumference**.

Python defines a variable when it is given a value for the first time, and *does not require a declaration*. The type of the variable is defined at that moment too; that is, if a number is assigned to a name, then that name is expected to represent a number from then on. If a string is assigned to a name, then that name will be expected to be a string from then on. Trying to use a variable before it has been given a value and a type is an error. Attempting the calculation:

```
area = side*side
```

is not allowed unless there is a variable named **side** already defined at this point. The following is OK because it defines **side** first, and then in turn is used to define **area**:

```
side = 12.0
area = side*side
```

The two lines above are called *statements* in Python, and a statement usually ends at the end of the line (the "enter" key was pressed). This is a bit unusual in a computer language, and people who already know Java or C++ have some difficulty with this idea at first. In other computer languages statements are separated by semicolons, not by the end of the line. In fact, in most languages the indenting of lines in the program does not have any meaning except to the programmer. *In Python indenting matters a great deal*, as will be seen shortly.

The expressions we use in assignments can be pretty complicated, but they are really only things that we learned in high school and are the same, essentially, as in Java. We can add, subtract, multiply, and divide. Precedence rules for math operations are the same as for Java: multiplication and division are performed before addition and subtraction, otherwise *evaluation is done left to right*, so 6/3*2 is 4 (do the division first) as opposed to 1 (if the multiplication was done first). These are rules that should be familiar because people are taught to do arithmetic in this way. The symbol "**" means exponent *or to the power of*, so **2**3** is 2^3 which is 8, and this operator has a higher precedence than (i.e., is done before) the others. Parentheses can be used to specify the order of things. So, for example, **(2+3)**2** is 25, because the expression within the parentheses is done first, then the exponent.

Exchanging Information with the Computer

When using most programming languages, it is necessary to design communication with the computer program. This goes two ways: the program will inform the user of things, such as the circumference of a circle given a specific radius, and the user may want to tell the program certain things, like the value of the radius for computing the circumference. We communicate with a program using *text*, which is to say characters typed into a keyboard. When a computer is presenting results, that text is often in the form of human language, messages as sentences. "The circumference is 62.831852" could be such a message. The sentence is actually composed by a programmer and has a number or collection of numbers embedded within it.

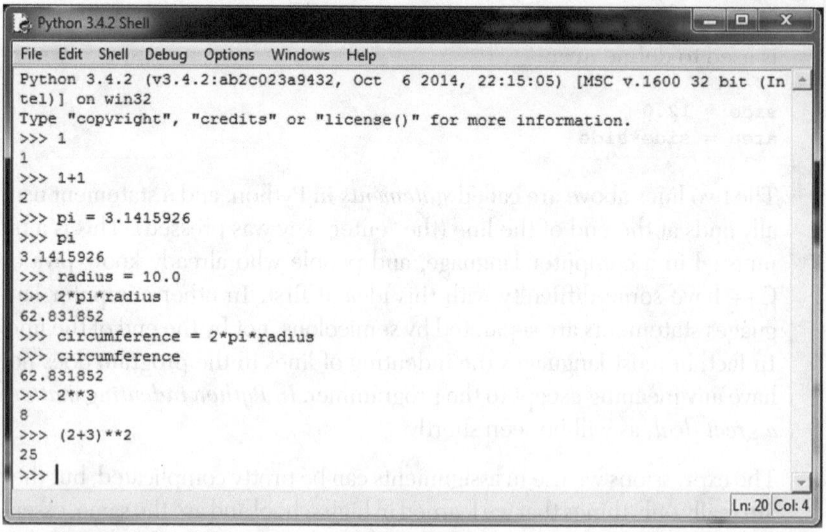

FIGURE 1.2. A Python GUI window showing the examples so far.

Java generally makes text I/O a little difficult, especially to and from files. Python allows a programmer to send a message to the screen, and hence to the user, using a **print** directive. This is the word **print** followed by a character string, which is often a set of characters in quotes. An example:

```
print ("The answer is yes.")
```

The parentheses are used to enclose everything that is to be printed; such a statement can print many strings if they are separated by commas. Numbers will be converted into strings for printing. So the following is correct:

```
print ("The circumference is ", 62.831852)
```

If a variable appears in the list following **print**, then the value of that variable will be printed, not the name of the variable. So:

```
print ("The circumference is ", circumference)
```

is also correct.

Example 1: Draw a Circle Using Characters

Assuming that it is desired to print a circle having a constant predefined radius, this can be done with a few print statements. The planning of the graphic itself (the circle) can be done using graph paper. Assuming that each character uses the same amount of space, a circle can be approximated using some skillfully placed "°" characters. Then print each row of characters using a print statement. A sample solution is:

```
print ("       ***          ")
print ("     ********        ")
print ("   *************      ")
print (" ***************     ")
print (" ***************     ")
print (" ***************     ")
print ("   *************     ")
print ("     ********        ")
print ("       ***          ")
```

Strings, Integers, and Real Numbers

A Python variable can hold either integers or real numbers (floats), but if a variable contains an integer then it is treated as an integer, and if it's holding a floating-point number then it is treated as one of those. What's the difference? First, there's a difference in how they are printed out. If we make the assignment **var = 1** and then print the value of **var**, it prints simply as 1. If we make the assignment **var = 1.0** and then print **var**, it prints as 1.0. In both cases **var** is a real or floating point number and will be treated as such. A variable can be first one thing and then another; it will be the last type it was assigned. Typed variables as seen in Java are not available in Python.

Arithmetic differs between integers and reals, but the only time that difference is really apparent is when doing division. Integers are always whole, non-fractional numbers. If we divide 3 by 2, both 3 and 2 are integers and so the division must result in an integer: the result is 1. This is because there is exactly a single 2 in 3, or if you like, 2 goes into 3 just once, with a remainder of 1. There is a specific operator for doing integer division: "*//*." So, 3*//*2 is equal to 1. The remainder part can't be handled and is discarded, but it can be found separately using the "%" operator. For example, 8*//*5 is 1, and 8%5 is the remainder, 3.

Of course fractions work fine for real numbers, and will be printed as decimal fractions: 8.0/5.0 is 1.6, for example. What happens if we mix reals and integers? In those cases things get converted into real, but now things get more complicated because order can matter a great deal. The expression 7*//*2*2.0 does the division 7*//*2 first, which is 3, and then multiplies that by 2.0, yielding the result 6.0; the result of 8/3*3.0 would be 5.333. Mixing integers and reals is not a good idea, but if done then the expressions should use parentheses to specify how the expression should be evaluated.

A real can be used in place of an integer in most places, but the result will be real. Thus, 2.0 * 3 = 6.0, not 6, and 6.0*//*2 is 3.0, not 3. There are some exceptions. To convert an integer to a real, there is a special operation named **float**: **float(3)** yields 3.0. Of course it's possible to simply multiply by 1.0, and the result will be float too. Converting float values to integers is more complicated, because of the fraction issue: what happens to the digits to the right of the decimal? The operation **int** will take a floating-point value and throw away the fraction. As a result, the value of **int(3.5)** will be 3. It's normal in human calculations to round to the nearest integer, and the operation **round(3.5)** does that, resulting in 4.

Number Bases

In Python numbers are given in decimal (base 10) by default. However, if a numeric constant begins with "0o" (zero followed by the letter "o"), Python assumes it is base 8 (octal). The number **0o21**, for example, is

$21_8 = 17_{10}$. A number that begins with "0x" is hexadecimal. **0x21** is $21_{16} = 33_{10}$. This applies only to integers.

There is a number base that is the most important, because it lies under all of the numbers on a computer. That would be base 2. All numbers on a modern digital computer are represented in base 2, or binary, in their internal representation. A binary number has only two digits, 0 and 1, and each represents a power of 2. Thus, 1101_2 is $1°2^3 + 1°2^2 + 0°2^1 + 1 = 8 + 4 + 1 = 13_{10}$. In Python a binary number begins with "0b," so the number **0b10101** represents 21_{10}.

Example 2: Compute the Circumference of Any Circle (Input)

When humans send information into a computer program, the data tends to be in the form of numbers, but humans use text as the means to communicate them. The Python code that was written to calculate the radius of a circle only did the calculation for a single radius: 10. That's not as useful as a program that computes the circumference of any circle, and that would mean allowing the user to tell the program what radius to use. This should be easy to do, because it is something that is needed frequently. Frequently needed things should always be easy. In the case of sending a number into a program in Python, the word **input** can be used. For example:

```
radius = input ()
```

will accept a number from the keyboard, typed by the user, and will return it as a string of characters. This makes sense because the user typed it as a string of characters, but it can't be used in a calculation in this form. To convert it into the internal form of a number, we must specifically ask for this to be done:

```
radius = input()
radius = float(radius)
```

will read a string into **radius**, then convert it into a *floating-point* (real) number and assign it to the variable **radius** again. This can be done all in one statement:

```
radius = float(input())
```

Now the variable radius can be used to calculate a circumference. This is a whole computer program that does a useful thing. If the value of **radius** was to be an integer, the code would read:

```
radius = int(input())
```

If the conversion to a number is not done, then Python will give an error message when the calculation is performed, as in the following:

```
Traceback (most recent call last):
  File "<pyshell#13>", line 1, in <module>
      circumference = 2*pi*radius
    TypeError: can't multiply sequence by non-int of
    type 'float'
```

This is pretty uninformative to a beginning programmer. What is a *Traceback*? What's *pyshell*? There are clues as to what this means, though. The line of code at which the error occurs is given and the term *TypeError* is descriptive. This error means that something that can't be multiplied (a string) was used in an expression involving a multiplication. That thing is the variable **radius** in this instance, because it was a text string and was not converted to a number.

Also note that **int(input())** can present problems when the input string does not in fact contain an integer. If it is a floating-point number, this results in an error. The expression **int("3.14159")** could be interpreted as an attempt convert the string containing *pi* into an integer, and would have the value 3; in fact it is an error. The function **int** was passed a *string* and the string contained a float, not an int. This is something of a quirk of Python. It is better to convert input numbers into floats.

A working program for this would be:

```
print ("This program finds the circumference of a circle.")
radius = input ("Enter the radius of the circle: ")
radius = float(radius)
circ = radius *2.0 * 3.1415926
print ("The circumference is ", circ)
```

IF Statements

The word "if" indicates a standard *conditional sentence* in English. The condition in the first case is the phrase "if the light is red" (called in English the *protaxis* or *antecedent*) and the consequence to that is the phrase "then stop" (the *apodosis* or *consequent*). Terminology aside, the intent is clear to an English speaker: on the condition that the light is red, then the necessary action is that the driver is to stop their car. The action is conditional on the antecedent, which in Python will be called an *expression* or, more precisely, a *logical expression*, which has the value **True** or **False**.

The structure or syntax of this sort of thing in Python would be:

```
if the light is red:
    stop
```

or more exactly:

```
if light == red:
    # execute whatever code makes the car stop
```

This is a Python **if** statement.

In Python an **if** statement begins with the word **if**, followed by an expression that evaluates to **True** or **False**, followed by a colon (:), and then a series of statements that are executed if the expression is true. The names **True** and **False** are constants having the obvious meaning, and a variable that can take on these values is a *logical* or *Boolean* variable. The expression is the only tricky part. It can be a constant like **True**, or a variable that has a **True** or **False** value, or a *relational expression* (one that compares two things) or a logical combination of any of these—anything that has a result that is true or false.

```
if True:            # Constant
if flag:            # Logical variable
if a < b:           # relational expression
if a<b and c>d:     # logical combination
```

A logical expression can be any arithmetical expression using any of the following operators:

<	Less than
>	Greater than
<=	Less than or equal to
>=	Greater than or equal to
==	Equal to
!=	Not equal to

Logical combinations can be:

and	e.g.:	a==b and b==c	
or	e.g.:	a==b or a==c	
not	e.g.:	not (a == b)	# same as !=

The syntax is simple and yet allows a huge number of combinations. For example:

```
if p == q and not p ==z and not z == p:
if pi**2 < 12:
if  (a**b)**(c-d)/3 <= z**3:
```

$$\textbf{if} \qquad \text{a<b} \qquad :$$

The key word, known by Python, that indicates this is an IF statement.	An expression that evaluates to **True** or **False**.	The colon indiates the end of the first part of the statement. Think iof it as meaning **THEN**, as in **IF expression THEN**

FIGURE 1.3. Syntax of an IF statement.

The *consequent*, or the actions to be taken if the logical expression is true, follows the colon on the following lines. The next statement is indented more than the **if**, and all statements that follow immediately that have the same indentation are a part of the consequent and are executed if the condition is true, otherwise none of them are. As an example, consider:

```
if a < b:
    a = a + 1
    b = b - 1
c = a - b
```

In this case the two statements following the ":" are indented four spaces past the **if** line. This tells Python that they are both part of the **if** statement, and that if the value of **a** is smaller than the value of **b**, then *both* of those statements will be executed. Python calls such a group of statements a *suite*. The assignment to the variable **c** is indented to the same level as the **if**, so it will be executed in any case and is not conditional.

The use of indentation to connect statements into groups is unusual in programming languages. Most languages in use pretty much ignore spaces and line breaks altogether, and use a statement separator such as a semicolon to demark statements. So, in the Java language the above code would look like this:

```
if (a<b) {
  a = a + 1;
  b = b - 1;
}
c = a - b;
```

The braces { . . . } enclose the suite, which would probably be called a *block* in Java or C++. Notice that this code is also indented, but in Java this means nothing to the computer. Indentation is used for clarity, so that someone reading the code later can see more clearly what is happening.

Semicolons are used in Python too, but much more rarely. If it is desired to place more than one statement on a single line, then semicolons can be used to separate them. The Python **if** statement under consideration here could be written as:

```
if a < b: a = a + 1; b = b -1
c = a - b
```

This is harder to comprehend quickly and is therefore less desirable. There are too many symbols all grouped together. A program that is easy to read is also easier to modify and maintain. Code is written for computers to execute, but also for humans to read.

There are some special assignment operators that can be used for incrementing and decrementing variables. In the above code the statement **a = a + 1** could be written as **a += 1**, and **b = b − 1** can be written as **b −= 1**. There is no real advantage to doing this, but other languages permit it so Python adopted it too. There is another syntax that can be used to simplify certain code in languages like Java and C, and that is the increment operator "++" and the decrement operator "—": ***Python does not have these.*** However, an effect of the way that Python deals with variables and expressions is that "++x" is legal; so is "++++x." The value is simply **x**. The expression "x++" is not correct.

Else

An **if** statement is a two-way or *binary* decision. If the expression is true, then the indicated statements are executed. If it is not true, then it is possible to execute a distinct set of statements. In one case the computer wins, and in the other the human wins. An *else* clause is what will allow this.

The ***else*** is not really a statement on its own, because it has to be preceded by an **if**, so it's part of the **if** statement. It marks the part of the statement that is executed only when the condition in the **if** is false. It consists of the word **else** followed by a colon, followed by a suite (sequence of indented statements). So a trivial example is:

```
if True:
    print ("The condition was true")
else:
    print ("the condition was false")
```

Note the indentation. The **else** as a clause is not required to accomplish any specific programming goals, and can be implemented using another **if**. The code:

```
if a < b:
    print ("a < b")
else:
    print ("a >= b")
```

could also be written as:

```
if a < b:
    print ("a < b")
if  not (a<b):
    print ("a >= b")
```

The **else** is *expressive, efficient*, and *syntactically convenient*. It is expressive because it represents a way that humans actually communicate. The word *else* means pretty much the same thing in Python as it does in English and Java.

Documentation

There are some problems with this program, but it does work. A large problem is that it always chooses the same number every time it is executed (that number being 7). This will be fixed later on. A less critical problem is that it is *undocumented*; that is, there are no instructions to a player concerning how to use the program and there is no description of how the program works that another programmer might use if modifying this code. This can be fixed by providing *internal* and *external* documentation.

External documentation is like a manual for the user. Most programs have such a thing, and even though this program is quite simple, some degree of documentation can be provided. In fact, it is brief enough that it could be printed whenever the program starts to run. For example:

```
print ("Rock-Paper_Scissors is a simple guessing game.")
print ("The computer will prompt you for your choice, ").
print ("which must be one of 'rock', 'paper', or 'scissors'")
print ("When you select a choice the computer will too (it ")
print ("will not cheat) and the winner is selected by three ")
print ("simple rules: rock beats scissors, paper beats ")
print ("rock, and scissors beat paper. It a tie happens")
print ("then you should play again.)
```

For many more sophisticated programs, such as *PowerPoint*, for example, the documentation is many pages and forms a small book. It would be distributed as a booklet along with the software or provided as a web site.

High-level languages like Python allow the programmer to add human language comments to the code that will be completely ignored by the computer, but that can be read by anyone looking at the code. These comments describe the action of the program, the meaning of the variables, details of computational methods used, and many other items of interest.

In Python a comment begins with the character "#" and ends at the end of the line. There are no rules for what can appear typed in a comment, but there are some guidelines developed through years of programming practice. A comment should not simply repeat what appears in the code; a comment should shed some light on an aspect of the program that might not be clear to everyone looking at it or document some of the history of the code, and it should be written in plain language. For instance:

```
# This program plays the game known as Rock-
# Paper-Scissors.
# Programmed by J. Parker Jan-2017
```

There is also something called a *docstring* that seems to do the same things as a comment, but covers multiple lines and is not really a comment. A *docstring* begins and ends with a triple quote:

```
print ("This code will execute")
"""
print ("This code is within a docstring")
"""
```

A *docstring* is actually a string, not a comment, but it behaves like a comment and can be used in that way. It can be especially useful for temporarily commenting out small sections of code while trying to find out where errors are. There are also programs that will collect the *docstrings* into a separate document that can be used as a description of the program. For that reason an intended use is to allow the programmer to explain the purpose of certain sections of code.

Rock-Paper-Scissors Again

With what is now known about Python, it is time to look at the rock-paper-scissors problem and see if it can be coded. It takes more steps, but it is really no more complicated that the guess-a-number program. The code is the same.

1) Select a choice from the three items: rock, paper, or scissors. Save this choice in a variable named **choice**.

A representation for the three items was decided upon when the solution was first described, where each choice was an integer. However, **input** reads strings, so it should be possible to avoid the conversion to numbers and use the strings directly.

```
choice = "paper"  # Computer chooses paper.
```

2) Ask the player for their choice.

Print as a prompt message.

```
print ("Rock-paper-scissors: type in your choice:    ")
```

3) Read the player's selection into a variable named **player**.

Use **input** as we did before, but this time read it as a string and keep it that way. The player must type either "rock," "paper," or "scissors," or else an error will be reported.

```
player = input ()
```

4) If **player** is equal to **choice**:

5)   Print the message "Game is a tie. Please try again."

Strings can be compared against each other for equality, so this step is quite simple:

```
if player == choice:
    print ("Game is a tie. Please try again.")
```

6) If **player** is equal to rock

7)   If **choice** is equal to scissors go to step 17

There will be no "go to step 17," but that step simply says that the player wins. Just print that message here.

```
if player == "rock":
    if choice == "scissors":
      print ("Congratulations. You win.")
    else:
      print ("Sorry - computer wins.")
```

8) If **player** is equal to paper

9)   If **choice** is equal to scissors go to step 17

```
if player == "paper":
    if choice == "scissors":
        print ("Sorry - computer wins.")
    else:
        print ("Congratulations. You win.")
```

10) If **player** is equal to scissors

11) If **choice** is equal to rock go to step 17

```
if player == "scissors":
    if choice == "rock":
        print ("Sorry - computer wins.")
    else:
        print ("Congratulations. You win.")
```

This code illustrates a new concept, if not a new language feature. It has **if** statements that are nested one within the other. Again, it's not necessary to do this because non-nested statements can implement the same decision. For example:

Nested **IF**s

```
if player == "scissors":

    if choice == "rock":
        print ("Computer wins.")

    else:
        print ("You win.")
```

Non-nested **IF**s

```
if player == "scissors
    and choice == "rock"
    print ("Computer wins")
if player == "scissors"
    and choice != "rock"
    print ("You win")
```

Nested **if** statements seem more expressive, and communicate the flow of the program better to a human programmer than does the non-nested code.

There is another Python language element that can be used here. Looking at the code, there is no indication when the user makes an error. For example, if the user enters "ROCK" (i.e., uppercase), then it will not match any of the choices and the program will not indicate this. In fact it won't print anything at all. What is really wanted is a sequence of **if-else-if-else** statements such as:

```
if player == "scissors":
    if choice == "rock":
else:
    if player == "rock":
        if choice == paper:
    else:
        if player == "scissors":
## and so on …
```

Python has a special feature that implements this nesting of **if** and **else**: the **elif**. The **elif** construct combines an **else** and an **if**, and this reduces the amount of indenting that has to be done. The following code snippets do the same thing:

```
if a<b:                    if a<b:
    print ("a<b")          'print ("a<b")
elif a>b:                  else:
    print ("a>b")          'if (a>b):
else:                          print ("a>b")
    print ("a=b")          else:
                               print ("a=b")
```

If too many nested if-else statements exist, then the indenting gets to be too much, whereas the **elif** allows the same indent level and has the same meaning.

Types Are Dynamic

To programmers who only program using Python, it would seem odd that a particular variable could have only one type, as is the case in C++, and that it would have to be initially defined to have that type, but it is true. In Python the type associated with a variable can change. For example, consider the statements:

```
x = 10                     # X is an integer
x = x*0.1                  # X is floating point now
x = (x*10 == 10)           # X is Boolean
```

Some find this perfectly logical, and others find it confusing. The fact is that so long as the variable is used according to its current type, all will be well.

It is also true that even apparently simple Python types can be quite complex in terms of their implementation. The point is that the programmer rarely needs to know about the underlying details of types like *integers*. In many programming languages an integer is simply a one- or two-word number, and the languages build operations like "+" from the instruction set of the computer. If, for example, a one-word integer A is added to another one B, it can be done using a single computer instruction like ADD A, B. This is very fast at execution time.

Python was designed to be convenient for the programmer, not fast. An integer is actually a complex object that has attributes and operations. This will become clearer as more Python examples are written and understood, but as a simple case think about the way that C++ represents an integer. It is a 32-bit (4-byte) memory location, which is a fixed-size space in memory. The largest number that can be stored there is $2^{32}-1$. Is that true in Python?

Here's a program that will answer that question, although it uses more advanced features:

```
for i in range (0,65):
    print (i, 2**i)
```

Even an especially long integer would be less than 65 bits. The fact is that this program runs successfully, and even rather quickly. *Integers in Python have an arbitrarily large size*. So calculating 2^{64} ° 2^{64} is possible and results in 340282366920938463463374607431768211456. This is very handy indeed from a programmer's perspective, if perhaps inefficient.

The type of a variable can be determined by the programmer as the program executes. The function **type()** will return the type of its parameter as a string, and can be printed or tested. So, the code:

```
z = 1
print (type(z))
z = 1.0
print(type(z))
```

will result in:

```
<class 'int'>
<class 'float'>
```

If one needed to know if **z** was a float at a particular moment, then:

```
if type(z)is float:
```

would do the trick. **Type(z)** does not return a string, it returns a *type*. The **print()** function recognizes that and prints a string, just as it does for **True** and **False**. So:

```
if type(z) == "<class 'float'>":
```

would be incorrect.

CHAPTER

2

REPETITION

One of the things that makes computers attractive to humans is their ability to do tedious, repetitive tasks accurately and at high speed without getting bored. Humans have to do things repeatedly, and not all of them can be done for us by computers. Brushing our teeth, driving to work, cleaning the carpet—all are repeated actions, and many would be called chores. In programming terms some might be referred to as *loops*.

Consider a Java **while** statement; the Python equivalent is very similar, except that instead of a compound statement being enclosed in braces it is indented, as before. The standard is four spaces, but any consistent number will do. All of the actions that follow the **while** are indented to indicate that they are a part of the activities to be repeated, just as was done in a Python **if** statement to mark the things that were to be done if the condition was true. This example illustrates one of the Python repetition structures quite accurately: the **while** statement.

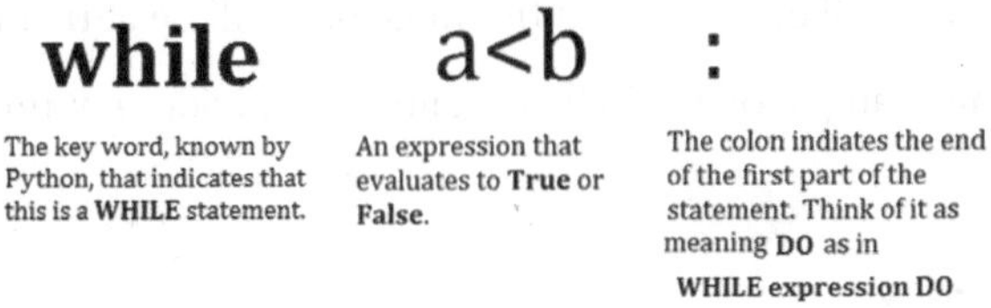

while   a<b   :

The key word, known by Python, that indicates that this is a WHILE statement.

An expression that evaluates to **True** or **False**.

The colon indiates the end of the first part of the statement. Think of it as meaning DO as in

WHILE expression DO

FIGURE 2.1. Essential syntax of the **WHILE** statement.

Note the lack of parentheses around the expression. Python does not require them.

The WHILE Statement

As in Java and C++, when using this repetition statement the condition is tested at the top or beginning of the loop. If upon that initial test the condition is true, then the body of the loop is executed; otherwise it is not, and the statement following the loop is executed. This means that it is possible that the code in the loop is not executed at all. The condition tested is the same kind of expression that is evaluated in an **if** statement: one that evaluates to **True** or **False**. It could be, and often is, a comparison between two numeric or string values, as it is in the example of Figure 2.1.

When the code in the body of the **while** statement has been executed, then the condition is tested again. If it is still true, then the body of the loop is executed again, otherwise the loop is exited and the statement following the loop is executed. There is an implication in this description that the body of the loop must change something that is used in the evaluation of the loop condition, otherwise the condition will always be the same and the loop will never terminate. So, here is an example of a loop that is entered and terminates:

```
a = 0
b = 0
while a < 10:
        a = a + 1
print (a)
```

The condition **a<10** is true at the outset because **a** has the value 0, so the code in the loop is executed. The lone statement in this loop increments **a**, so that after the first time the loop is executed the value of **a** is 1. Now the condition is tested and, again, **a<10** so the loop executes again. In the final iteration of the loop, the value of **a** starts out as 9, is incremented, and becomes 10. When the condition is tested it fails, because **a** is no longer less than 10 (it is equal), and so the loop ends. The statement following the loop is **print (a)**, and the value printed is 10. This loop explicitly modifies one of the variables in the loop condition, and it is easy to see that the loop will end and what the value of **a** will be at that time.

Here is an example of a loop that is entered and does *not* terminate:

```
a = 0
b = 0
while b < 10:
        a = a + 1
print (a)
```

In this case the value of **b** is less than 10 at the outset so the loop is entered. The body of the loop increments **a** as before, but does not change **b**.

The loop condition does not depend on **a**, only on **b**, so when the loop condition is tested again the value of **b** is still 0, and the loop executes again. The value of **b** will always be 0 each time it is tested, so the loop condition will always be true and the loop will never end. The print statement will never be executed.

Here is an example of a loop that is not entered:

```
a = 100
b = 0
while a < 10:
      a = a + 1
print (a)
```

The condition **a<10** is false at the outset because **a** has the value 100, so the code in the loop is not executed. The statement following the loop is executed next, which is the print statement, and the value printed is 100.

These loops are merely examples that illustrate the three possibilities for a **while** loop and do not calculate anything useful. The example from the previous chapter can make practical use of a while loop, and it would be useful to look at it again.

Modules and Random Numbers

Most games and simulations depend on an element of unpredictability or chance. We can use a random number to simulate real situations, which are complex enough that they *seem* random: the distance between cars on the freeway, or the number of customers in a store are examples.

Numbers are random only with respect to each other. Is the number "6" random? That's not really a good question. Is the sequence 87394 random? Perhaps a test could be devised to answer that. Is the sequence 66666 random? Most would say not, but it has the same probability of being generated at random as does 87394. To create good games and simulations, it is necessary to devise ways to generate a random number using a computer, and to test numbers to see if they are in fact random. Then it would be possible to simulate the flipping of a coin, or the rolling of a die.

Python encompasses the idea of a *module*, which provides a collection of functions that perform operations within a specified domain. These are Python functions that reside in a file, and it means that the name of the module has to be known as well as the names of the built-in functions within it. As one example, common mathematical functions are located within the module **math** and can be used by requesting the math module with the statement:

```
import math
```

Using a function in the math module involves using the name math followed by a period (".") followed by the name of the function. The "." opens the module so that the names within can be used, because there may be other built-in functions or even variables that have the same name. So, if the statements:

```
x = math.sqrt(64)
print (x)
```

are executed, the program will print the number 8, which is the square root of 64. The expression **sqrt(64)** is a *function call*, and executes the code needed to calculate the square root of 64. The name **sqrt** is the name of the function, which is code provided by the Python language. This particular call will always return the value 8, because 8 is always the square root of 64. It is very much like the functions that are studied in grade school mathematics, such as **sine** and **cosine**. A module can be thought of as a bag of programs. Each bag contains a set of programs that do a particular class of things, like mathematics or drawing. By specifying the name of the module, access to all of the functions within is granted, and by specifying the specific name of a function, the code that we want is specifically made available.

By the way, the **import** statement should be at the very beginning of the program.

It is possible to have a function that produces a random number as a value. It is in the module named **random**, and the function is called **random** too. For example:

```
import random
print ( random.random() )
```

Every time (well *almost* every time, because it *is* random, after all) the function is used, it will give a different value, a random value.

This code prints the value 0.07229650795715237. Why? Because **random. random()** produces a random number between 0.0 and 1.0. This is the most common example of a random number function, and is really very general. It's the same in Java. Increasing the range is done simply by multiplying by the maximum value desired; **random.random()*100** gives a random number between 0 and 100, for instance.

What if the problem is to simulate the roll of a die? The bag of code that is the **random** module contains other functions related to the generation of random numbers, and one of them is especially suited to this problem. A die roll would be implemented as:

```
random.randint (1, 6)
```

The **randint** function accepts two numbers, called *parameters*. The first is the lower limit of the range of random integers to be produced, and the second is the upper limit. Specifying 1 as the lower limit and 6 as the upper, as in the example above, means that it will generate numbers between 1 and 6 inclusive, which is what would be expected from rolling a die. The result of rolling two dice would be a number between 2 and 12, found by **random.randint(1,6) + random.randint (1,6)** (not random. randint(2,12) for reasons of mathematics).

Flipping a coin is a two-level choice, and could be done with **random. randint(1,2)**. More completely:

```
if (random.randint(1,2) == 1):
    print ("Heads")
else:
    print ("Tails").
```

The introduction of a random choice is a little more complicated for the rock-paper-scissors program because the variable holding the player's choice is a string. There are three possible choices, so to select one at random might look like this:

```
i = random.randint(1,3)
if i == 1:
    choice = "rock"
elif i == 2:
    choice = "paper"
else:
    choice = "scissors"
```

Many of the examples that will be developed will involve a game or puzzle of some kind, so the use of random numbers will be a consistent feature of the code shown.

Counting Loops

The **while** loop is obviously useful, and is in fact the only kind of loop that is required in order to implement any program. However, loops that involve counting a certain number of iterations are pretty common, and adding syntax for this kind of thing would be certain to be valuable for a programmer. Such a construct is the **for** loop. In some languages a **for** loop involves a special syntax, but in Python it involves a new type as well (a class of types, really): a *tuple*. Here is an example of a **for** loop:

```
for i in (1,2,3,4,5):
    print (i)
```

This will print the numbers 1 2 3 4 5, each on a separate line. The variable **i** takes on each of the values in the collection provided in parentheses and the loop executes once for each value of **i**. The collection (1,2,3,4,5) is called a *tuple*, and it can contain any Python objects in any order. It's basically just a set of objects. The following are legal *tuples*:

```
(3,6, 9, 12)
(2.1, 3.5, 9.1, 0, 12)
("green", "yellow", "red")
("red", 3, 4.5, 2, "blue", i)
                    #where i is a variable with a value
```

The **for** loop has the loop control variable (in the case above it is **i**) take on each of the values in the tuple, in left to right order, then executes the connected suite. The loop will therefore execute same the number of times as there are elements in the tuple.

Sometimes it may be necessary to have the loop execute a great many times. If the loop was to execute a million times, it would be more than awkward to require a program to list a million integers in a tuple. Python provides a function to make this more convenient: **range()**. It returns a tuple that consists of all of the integers between the two parameters it is given, including the lower endpoint. So:

```
range (1,10)   is (1,2,3,4,5,6,7,8,9)
range (-1, 2) is (-1, 0, 1)
range (-1, -3) is not a proper range.
range (1, 1000000) if the set of all integers from 1 to 9999999
```

Ranges involving strings are not allowed, although tuples having strings in them are certainly allowed. The original example for the loop can now be written:

```
for i in range(1,6):
    print i
```

and the loop that is to execute a million times could be specified as:

```
for i in (0, 1000000):
    print i
```

This would print the integers from 0 to 999999. If **range()** is passed only a single argument, then the range is assumed to start at 0; this means that **range (0,10)** and **range (10)** are the same.

for	i	in	(2,7,8)	:
The key word, known by Python, that indicates that this is a **for** statement.	A variable, the *loop control variable*, that will take on values in a given sequence.	The key word **in**, which is basically a placeholder	A **tuple** (or other sequence type) that enumerates the values the variable will take.	The colon indicates the end of the first part of the statement. Think of it as meaning **do** as in: **for i in (2,7,8) do**

FIGURE 2.2. The structure of a FOR statement.

Prime or Non-Prime

Here's a game that can illustrate the use of a **for** loop, and some other ideas as well. The computer presents the player with large numbers, one at a time. The player has to guess whether each number is *prime* or *non-prime*. A prime number does not have any divisors except 1 and itself. Examples of prime numbers are 3, 5, 11, and 17. The game ends either when a specific number of guesses have been made, or when the player makes a specific number of mistakes.

A key problem to solve in this game is to determine when a number is prime. The computer must be able to determine whether the player is correct, and so for any given number, there must be a way to figure out whether it is prime. Otherwise, the program for this game is not very complicated:

```
while game is not over:
    select a random integer k
    print k and ask the player if it is prime
    read the player's answer
    if player's answer is correct:
        print "You are right"
    else:
        print "You are wrong."
```

The mysterious portion of this program is the **if** statement that asks if the player's answer is correct. This really means that the program must determine whether or not the number K is prime and then see if the player agrees. How can it be determined that a number is prime? A prime number has no divisors, so if one can be found then the number is not prime. The *modulo* operator % can be used to tell if a division has a remainder: if k % n = 0 then the number n divides evenly into k, and k is not prime.

So to find out whether a number is prime, try dividing it by all numbers smaller than it, and if any of them have a zero remainder then the number is not prime. This is a job for a **for** loop. Here's a first draft:

```
isprime = True
for n in range (1, K):
    if k%n == 0:
        isprime = False
```

After the loop has completed, the variable **isprime** indicates whether K is prime or not. This seems pretty simple, if tedious. It does a lot of divisions. Too many, in fact, because it is not possible for any number larger than K/2 to divide evenly into K. So a slightly better program would be:

```
isprime = True              # Is the number K prime?
for n in range (1, int(k/2)) # Divide K by all numbers < K/2
    if k%n == 0:             # If the remainder is 0 then n
        isprime = False      # divides evenly into K:
                                 not prime
# If isprime is still true here then the number is prime.
```

Next, this section of program should be incorporated into a complete program that plays the game. If the game is supposed to allow 10 guesses, then the first step is to repeat the whole thing 10 times:

```
import random
correct = 0                  # The number of correct guesses
for iteration in range(0, 10):  # 10 guesses
```

Now select a number at random. It should be large enough so that it is hard to see immediately if it is prime, although even numbers are a giveaway:

```
K = random.randint(10000, 1000000)    # Generate a new number
```

Next print a message to the user asking for their guess and read it:

```
print ("Prime or Not: Is the number ",K," prime? (yes or no)")
answer = input()       # Read the user's choice
```

The user types in a string, "yes" or "no," as their response. The variable **isprime** that was used in the program that determines whether K is prime is logical, being **True** or **False**. It could be made into a string too so that it was the same as what the user typed, and then it could be compared directly against the user's input:

```
isprime = "yes"
```

Now comes the code for determining primality as coded above, except with **isprime** as a string:

```
isprime = True               # Is the number K prime?
for n in range (1, int(k/2)) # Divide K by all numbers < K/2
    if k%n == 0:             # If the remainder is 0 then n
        isprime = "no"       # divides evenly into K:
                               not prime
# If isprime is still true here then the number is prime.
```

At this point the variable **isprime** is either "yes" or "no" depending on whether K is actually prime. The user's guess is also "yes" or "no." If they are equal then the user guessed correctly.

```
if isprime==answer:
    print ("You are correct!")
    correct = correct + 1
else:
    print ("You are incorrect.")
```

Finally, the outer loop is ended and the result is printed. The value of the variable **correct** is the number of correct guesses the user made, because it was incremented every time a correct answer was detected. The last statement is:

```
print ("You gave ",correct," right answers out of 10.")
```

Exiting from a Loop

A clever programmer would notice a pretty serious inefficiency with the prime number program. When it has been determined that the number is not prime, the loop continues to divide more numbers into **k** until **k/2** of them have been tried. If k= 999992 then it is known after the first iteration that the number is not prime; it is even, so it can't be prime. But the program continues to try nearly another half million numbers anyway. What is needed is a way to tell the program that the loop is over. There is a way to do this.

A loop can be exited using the **break** statement. It is simply the word **break** by itself. The correct way to use this in the program above would be:

```
for n in range (1, int(k/2))   # Divide K by all numbers< K/2
    if k%n == 0:               # If the remainder is 0 then n
        isprime = "no"         # divides evenly into K: not prime
        break
```

This loop terminates when the number **k** is known to be not prime. The statement following the loop will be executed next. This can save a lot of computer cycles, but does not make the program more correct—just faster.

A variation on this is the **continue** statement. This will result in the next iteration of the loop being started without executing any more statements in the current iteration. This avoids doing a lot of work in a loop after it is known it's not necessary. For example, doing some task for a bunch of names except for people named "Smith" could use a continue statement:

```
for name in
('Jones','Smith','Peters','Sinatra','Bohr','Conrad'):
    print (name);
    if name == 'Smith':
        continue
# Now do a bunch of stuff . . .
```

Both **break** and **continue** do the same thing in both **while** and **for** loops.

Modifying the loop variable will not change the number of iterations the loop will execute. In fact, it has no effect. This loop demonstrates that:

```
for i in range(0, 10):
    print ("Before ",i)
    i = i + 1000
    print ("After ",i)
```

It prints:

```
Before  0
After   1000
Before  1
After   1001
      .  .  .
```

and so on. It seems that the value of **i** changes after the assignment for the remainder of the loop and then is set to what it should be for the next iteration. This makes sense if Python is treating the range as a set of elements (it is), and it assigns the next one to **i** at the beginning of each iteration. Unlike a **while** loop, there is not a test for continuation. In any case, changing **i** here does not alter the number of iterations and can't be used in place of a **break**.

Else

The idea that the loop can be exited explicitly makes the normal termination of the loop something that should be detectable too. When a **while** or **for** loop exits normally by exhausting the iterations or having the expression become **False**, it is said to have *fallen through*. When the **for** loop in the prime number program detects a factor, it executes a **break** statement, thus exiting the loop. What if it never does that? In that case no factor exists, and the number is prime. The program as it stands has a flag that indicates this, but it could be done with an **else** clause on the loop.

The **else** part of a **while** or **for** loop is executed only if the loop falls through; that is, when it is not exited through a **break**. This can be quite useful, especially when the loop is involved in a search, as will be discussed later. In the case of the prime number program, an **else** could be used when the number is in fact prime, as follows:

```
for n in range (1, int(k/2))   # Divide K by all numbers< K/2
    if k%n == 0:               # If the remainder is 0 then n
        isprime = "no"         # divides evenly into K:
        break                      not prime
else:
    isprime = "yes"            # Loop not exited: it is prime
```

An **else** in a **while** loop occurs when the condition becomes false. Consider a loop that reads from input until the user types "end" and is searching for the name "Smith":

```
inp = input()
while (inp != "Smith"):
    s = input()
    if s == "end":
        break
else:
    print ("Smith was found")
# When the program reaches this point it is no
# longer known whether Smith was found.
```

Of course, the **else** is not required, and some programmers believe it is even harmful. There are always other ways to accomplish the same thing.

Exceptions and Errors

A correct program depends on the programmer being able to identify all possible circumstances that can occur and knowing how to deal with each of them. Failing to handle one possible situation is an error, and the program will behave unpredictably if that situation occurs in practice. Statements that handle errors appear all through real (commercial) code. In fact, it is common that there are more statements that detect and deal with errors than code that actually computes an answer.

User input is a frequent cause of mistakes in programs. It's not that the user is the problem; the programmer must anticipate all possible ways that a user can enter data. There is usually one correct way but many erroneous ones, and it is impossible to predict what a user will enter from a keyboard in response to any request. Similarly, the contents of a file may not be what the programmer expects. File formats are standards, but sometimes there are variations, and at other times a user may have entered the data improperly. While the mistake is on the part of the user, it is also a programming mistake if the error is not detected and is allowed to have an impact of the execution of the program.

Most modern languages, Python included, have implemented a way to catch errors and permit the programmer to handle them without having tests before each statement or expression. This facility is called the *exception*.

The word *exception* communicates a way to think about how errors will be handled. Some code is legal and calculates a desired value *except* under certain circumstances, or *unless* some particular thing happens. The way it works is that the program tries to perform some operation and errors are allowed to occur. If one does, the computer hardware or operating system detects it and tells Python. The program cannot continue in the way that was planned, which is why this is called an exception. The programmer can tell Python what to do if specific errors occur by writing some code that deals with the problem. If the programmer did not do this, then the default is for Python to print an error message that describes the error and then stop executing the program. Error messages can be seen as a failure on the part of the programmer to handle errors correctly.

A simple example is the divide by zero error mentioned previously. If the expression **a/b** is to be evaluated, the value of **b** can be checked to make sure it is not zero before the division is done:

```
if b != 0:
    c = a/b
```

This can be tedious for the programmer if a lot of calculations are being done, and can be error prone. The programmer may forget to test one or two expressions, especially if engaged in modifications or testing. Using exceptions is a matter of allowing the error to happen and letting the system test for the problem. The syntax is as follows:

```
try:
      c = a/b
except:
      c = 1000000
```

The **try** statement begins a section of code within which certain errors are being handled by the programmer's code. After that statement, code is indented to show that it is part of the **try** region. Nearly any code can appear here, but the **try** statement must be ended before the program ends.

The **except** statement consists of the keyword **except** and, optionally, the name of an error. The errors are named by the Python system, and the correct name has to be used, but if no error name is given as in this example, then any error will cause the code in the **except** statement to be executed. Not specifying a name here is an implicit assumption that either only one kind of error could possibly occur or that no matter what error happens, the same code will be used to deal with it. Specifying an unrecognized name is itself an error. The name can be a variable, but that variable must have been assigned a recognized error name before the error occurs. The code following the **except** keyword is indented too, to show that it is part of the **except** statement. This is referred to by programmers as an *error handler*, and it is executed only if the specified error occurs.

This appears to be even more verbose than testing **b**, but any number of statements can appear between the **try** and the **except**. This section of code is now protected from divide-by-zero errors. If any occur then code following the **except** statement will be executed; otherwise that code will not execute. If other errors occur then the default action will take place—an error message will be printed.

Testing specifically for the divide-by-zero error can be done by specifying the correct error name in the **except** statement:

```
try:
      c = a/b
except ZeroDivisionError:
      c = 1000000
```

More than one specific error can be caught in one **except** statement:

```
try:
    c = a/b
except (ValueError, ZeroDivisionError):
    c = 1000000
```

Clearly (**ValueError, ZeroDivisionError**) is a tuple, and could be made longer and could be assigned to a variable.

Also, there can be many **except** statements associated with a single **try**:

```
try:
    c = a/b
except ValueError:
    c = 0
exceptZeroDivisionError:
    c = 1000000
```

And, as was mentioned, a variable can hold the value of the error to be caught:

```
k = ZeroDivisionError
try:
    c = a/b
except k:
    c = 1000000
```

Finally, the exception name can be left out altogether. In that case any exception that occurs will be caught and the exception code will be executed:

```
try:
    c = a/b
except:
    c = 0
```

CHAPTER 3

SEQUENCES: STRINGS, TUPLES, AND LISTS

I t was mentioned in Chapter 2 that **for** loops in Python are different from those found in many other languages in that they use a tuple to define the values that will be assigned to the control variable. Tuples are useful in many situations, and are only one example of a wider range of data types that includes *strings*, *tuples*, and *lists* as objects that consist of multiple parts. They are called *sequence* types. An integer or a float is a single number, whereas a sequence type consists of a collection of items, each of which is a number or a character. Each member of a sequence is given a number based on its position: the first element in the sequence is given 0, the second is 1, and so on. This is a fundamental data structure in Python and has influenced the syntax of the language.

Strings

A *string* is a sequence of characters. The word *sequence* implies that the order of the characters within the string matters, and that is certainly true. Strings most often represent the way that communication between a computer and a human takes place. The order of the characters within a word matters a great deal to a human because some sequences are words and others are not. The string "last" is a word, but "astl" is not. Also, the strings "salt" and "slat" are words and use exactly the same characters as "last" but in a different order.

Because order matters, the representation of a string on a computer will impose an order on the characters within, and so there will be a first character, a second, and so on, and it should be possible to access each character individually. A string will also have a *length*, which is the number of characters within it. A computer language will provide specific things that can be done to something that is a string: these are called operations, and a type is defined at least partly by what operations can be done to something of that type. Because a string represents text in the human sense, the operations on strings should represent the kinds of things that would be done to text. This would include printing and reading, accessing any character, linking strings into longer strings, searching a string for a particular word, and so on.

String constants are simply characters enclosed in either single or double quotes, similar to those in Java. Assigning a string constant to a variable causes that variable to have the string type and gives it a value. So the statements:

```
name = "John Doe"
address = '121 Second Street'
```

cause the variables **name** and **address** to be strings with the assigned value. Note that either type of quote can be used, but a string that begins with a double quote must end with one.

A string behaves as if its characters are stored as consecutive characters in memory. The first character in a string is at location or index 0, and can be accessed using square brackets after the string name. Using the definitions above, name[0] is "J" and name[5] = "D." If an index is specified that is too large, it results in an error because it amounts to an attempt to look past the end of the string.

How many characters are there in the string **name**? The built-in function **len()** will return the length of the string. The largest legal index is one less than this value: the first character of a string **name** has index 0, and the final one has index 7; the length is 8. Thus, any index between 0 and **len(name)-1** is legal. The following code prints all of the characters of **name** and can be thought of as the basic pattern for code that scans through the characters in strings:

```
for i in range(0, len(name)):
    print (name[i], end="")
```

This may be a little confusing, but remember that the **range(0,n)** does not include **n**. This loop runs through values of **i** from 0 to **len(name)-1**.

Some languages have a *character* type, but Python does not. A string of length one is what Python uses instead. A component of a string is therefore another string. The first character of the string **name**, which is **name[0]**, is "J," the string containing only one character.

Comparing Strings

Two strings can be compared in the same manner as two integers or real numbers, by using one of the relational operators ==, !=, <, >, <=, or >=. What it means for two strings to be equal is simple and reasonable: if each corresponding character in two strings is the same, then the strings are equal. That is, for strings **a** and **b**, if **a[0] == b[0]**, and **a[1]==b[1],** and so on to the final character **n**, and **a[n] == b[n]**, then the two strings **a** and **b** are equal and **a==b**. Otherwise **a!=b**. By the way, this implies that equal strings have the same length.

What about inequalities? Strings in real life are often sorted in alphabetical order. Names in a telephone book, files in a doctor's office, and books in a store: these tend to appear in a logical order based on the alphabet. This is also true in Python. The string "abc" is less than the string "def," for example. Why? Because the first letter in "abc" comes before the first letter in "def"; in other words, "abc"[0] < "def"[0]. Yes, characters in string constants can be accessed using their index.

A string **s1** is less than string **s2** if all characters from 0 through **k** in the two strings are equal, and **s1[k+1]<s2[k+1]**. So the following statements are true:

```
"abcd" < "abce"
"123" < "345"
"ab" < "abc"
```

In the last example, the space character " " is smaller than (i.e., comes before) the letter "c." What if the strings are not the same length? The string "ab" < "abc", so if two strings are equal to the end of one of them, then the shorter one is considered to be smaller. These rules are consistent so far with those taught in grade school for alphabetization. Trailing spaces do not matter. *Leading* spaces can matter, because a space comes before any alphabetic character; that is, " " < "a". Thus "ab" > " z".

As an example that compares strings, consider the following:

```
a = "J"
b = "j"
c = "1"
if b<c:
    print ("Lcase < numbers")
```

```
else:
    print("Lcase > numbers")
if a<c:
    print ("Ucase < numbers")
else:
    print("Ucase > numbers")
```

This results in the output:

```
Lcase > numbers
Ucase > numbers
```

Problem: Does a City Name, Entered at the Console, Come before or after the Name *Denver*?

This involves reading a string and comparing it against the constant string "Denver." Let the input string be read into a variable named **city**. Then the answer is:

```
city = input()
if city < "Denver":
    print ("The name given comes before Denver in an
alphabetic list")
elif city > "Denver":
    print ("The name given comes after Denver in an alphabetic
list")
else:
    print ("The name given was Denver")
```

If "Chicago" is typed at the console as input, the result is:

```
Chicago
The name given comes before Denver in an alphabetic list
```

However, if case is ignored and "chicago" is typed instead, then the result is:

```
chicago
The name given comes after Denver in an alphabetic list
```

because, of course, the lowercase "c" comes (as do *all* lowercase letters) after the upper case "D" at the beginning of "Denver."

Slicing – Extracting Parts of Strings

To a person a string usually contains words and phrases, which are smaller parts of a string. Identifying individual words is important. To Python this is true also. A Python program consists of statements that contain individual words and character sequences that each have a particular meaning. The words "if," "while," and "for" are good examples. Individual characters can be referenced through indexing, but can words or collections of characters be accessed? Yes, if the location (index) of the word is known.

Problem: Identify a "print" Statement in a String

The statement:

```
print ("Lcase < numbers")
```

appears in the previous example program. This can be thought of as a string, and assigned to a variable:

```
statement = 'print ("Lcase < numbers")'
```

Question: is this a **print** statement? It is if the first five characters are the word "print." Each of those characters could be tested individually, but that would be pretty ugly. Python offers a nicer way to do it. A *slice* is a set of continuous characters within a string. This means their indices are consecutive, and they can be accessed as a sequence by specifying the range of indices within brackets. The previous situation concerning the print statement could be done like this:

```
if statement[0:5] == "print":
```

The slice here does not include character 5, but it is 5 characters long including characters 0 through 4 inclusive. A slice from **i** to **j** (i.e., **x[i:j]**) does not include the character at location **j**. This means that the following lines produce the same result:

```
fname[0]
fname[0:1]
```

If the first index is omitted, then the start index is assumed, so the statement:

```
if statement[0:5] == "print":
```

is the same as:

```
if statement[:5] == "print":
```

If the second index is omitted, then the last legal index is assumed, which is to say the index of the final character. So the assignment:

```
str = statement[6:]
```

results in the value of **str** being "(**Lcase < numbers**)." Both indices can be omitted, which does sound silly, but really just means from the first to the last character, or the entire string.

Editing Strings

Python does *not* allow the modification of individual parts of a string. That is, things like:

```
str[3] = "#"
str[2:3] = ".."
```

are *not* allowed. So how can strings be modified? For example, consider the string variable:

```
fname = "image"
```

If this is supposed to be the name of a JPG image file, then it must end with the suffix ".jpg."

Problem: Create a JPEG File Name from a Basic String

The string **fname** can be edited to end with ".jpg" in a few ways, but the easiest one to use is the concatenation operator "+."

To *concatenate* means "to link or join together." If the variables **a** and **b** are strings, then **a+b** is the string consisting of all characters in **a** followed by all characters in **b**; the operator "+" in this context means to concatenate, rather than numerical addition. The designers of Python and many other languages that implement this operator think of concatenation as string addition.

To use this to create the image file name, simply concatenate ".jpg" to the string **fname**:

```
fname = fname + ".jpg"
```

The result is that the new value of **fname** is "image.jpg."

File suffixes are very often the subject of string manipulations and provide a good example of string editing. For instance, given a file name stored as a string variable **fname**, is the suffix ".jpg"? Based on the preceding discussion, the question can be answered using a simple **if** statement:

```
if fname[len(fname)-4:len(fname)] == '.jpg':
```

Using a slice it could also take the form:

```
if fname[len(fname)-4:] == ".jpg"
```

A valuable thing to know is that negative indices index from the *right*-hand side of the string; that is, from the end. So **fname[-1]** is the final character in the string, **fname[-2]** is the one previous to that, and so on. The last four characters, the suffix, would be captured by using **filename[-4:]**.

Problem: Change the Suffix of a File Name

Some individuals use the suffix ".jpeg" instead of ".jpg." Some programs allow this; others do not. Some code that would detect and change this suffix would be:

```
if fname[len(fname)-5:] == ".jpeg":  # identfy jpeg suffix
    fname = fname[0:len(fname)-5]    # remove the last 5 char
    fname = fname + ".jpg"           # append correct suffix
```

Problem: Reverse the Order of Characters in a String

There are things about any programming language that could be considered to be 'idioms.' These are things that a programmer experienced in the use of that language would consider normal use, but that others might consider odd. This problem exposes a Python idiom. Given what is known so far about Python, the logical approach to string reversal might be as follows:

```
# city has a legal value at this point
k = len(city)
for i in range(0,len(city)):
    city = city + city[k-i-1]
city = city[len(city)//2:]
```

This reverses the string named **city** that exists prior to the loop and creates the reversed string. An experienced Python programmer would do this differently. The syntax for taking a slice has a variation that has not been discussed; a third parameter exists. A string slice can be expressed as:

```
myString[a:b:c]
```

where **a** is the starting index, **b** is the final index+1, and **c** is the increment. If:

```
str = "This string has 30 characters."
```

then str[0:30:2] is "Ti tighs3 hrces," which is every second character. The increment represents the way the string is sampled, that is, at each **increment** the character is copied into the result. Most relevant to the current example, the increment can be negative. The idiom for reversing a string is:

```
print (str[::-1])
```

As has been explained, the value of str[:] is the whole string. Specifying an increment of -1 implies that the string is scanned from 0 to the end, but in reverse order. This is not intuitive, but it is probably the way that an experienced Python programmer would reverse a string. Any programmer should use the parts of any language that they comprehend very well, and should keep in mind the likely skill set of the people likely to read the code.

Problem: Is a Given File Name That of a Python Program?

A Python program terminates with the suffix '.py.' An obvious solution to this problem is to simply look at the last three characters in the string **s** to see if they match that suffix:

```
if  s[len(s)-3:len(s)] == '.py':
    print ("This is a Python program.")
```

Perhaps. But is "PROGRAM.PY" a legal Python program? It happens that it is. So is "program.Py" and "program.pY." What can be done here?

String Methods

A good way to do the test in this case is to convert the suffix to all upper- or all lowercase before doing the comparison. Comparing against ".py" means converted to lowercase, which is done by using a built-in *method* named **lower**:

```
s1 = s[len(s)-3:len(s)]
if  s1.lower()== '.py':
    print ("This is a Python program.")
```

The variable **s1** is a string that will contain the final three characters of **s**. The expression **s1.lower()** creates a copy of **s1** in which all characters are lowercase. It's called a *method* to distinguish it from a function, but they are very similar things. You should recall that a method is simply a function that belongs to one type or class of objects. In this case **lower()** belongs to the type (or class) *string*. There could be another method named **lower()** that belongs to another class that does a completely different thing. The dot notation indicates that it is a method, and what class it belongs to: the same class of things that the variable belongs to. In addition, the variable itself is really the first parameter; if **lower** were a function, then it might be called by **lower(s1)** instead of **s1.lower()**. In the latter case the "." is preceded by the first parameter.

Strings all have many methods, and these can be found online or in most Python texts. In the table below the variable **s** is the *target* string, the one being operated upon. This means that the method names below will appear following "s."—for example, **s.lower()**. Let the value of **s** be given by **s = "hello to you all."** These methods are intended to provide the operations needed to make the string type in Python function as a major communication device from humans to a program.

capitalize() – Returns the target string but with the first letter capitalized.

count(str,beg=0,end=len(s)) – Returns a count of how many times the string str occurs in the target. If values for beg and end are given, then the count is performed using only character indices between beg and end.

endswith(suffix, beg=0, end=len(s)) – Returns True if the target string ends with the given suffix and return False otherwise. If beg and end are given, then do the test on the substring between beg and end.

find(str,beg=0end=len(string)) – If the string str appears with the target string, then return the index at which it occurs; return -1 if it does not occur. If beg and end are provided, then use the substring from beg to end.

isdigit() – Returns True if the target string contains only digits and False otherwise.

islower() – Returns True if the target string has at least one alphabetic character and all alphabetic characters are lowercase. Return False otherwise.

isspace() – Returns True if the target string contains only whitespace characters and returns False otherwise.

isupper() – Returns True if s has at least one alphabetic character and all alphabetic characters are uppercase. Returns False otherwise.

lower() – Converts all uppercase letters in string to lowercase.

replace(old, new [, max]) – Replaces all occurrences of the string old in the target with the string new. If max is specified, replace at most max instances.

split (str="", num=string.count(str)) – Returns a list of substrings obtained from the target using str as a delimiter. Space is the default for str. Subdivide at most num times if that is specified.

splitlines (num=string.count('\n')) – Splits the target string at all (or num, if it is specified) NEWLINEs and returns a list of each line with the NEWLINEs removed.

upper() – Converts the lowercase letters in the string to uppercase.

Spanning Multiple Lines

Text as seen in human documents may contain many characters, even multiple lines and paragraphs. A special delimiter, the *triple quote*, is used when a string constant is to span many lines. This has been mentioned previously in the context of multiline comments. The regular string delimiters will terminate the string at the end of the line. The triple quote consists of either of the two existing delimiters repeated three times. For example, to assign some Python code to the variable **code**:

```
code = """list = [1,2,4,7,12,15,21]
for i in list:
    print(i, i*2)"""
```

When **code** is printed the line endings appear where they were placed in the constant. This example is a particularly good one in that most Python programs require that lines end precisely where the programmer intended.

This program can be executed, too; the following statement will actually execute the code in the string:

```
exec (code)
```

For Loops Using Strings

Earlier in this section a **for** loop was written to print each character in the string. That loop was:

```
for i in range(0, len(name)):
    print (name[i], end="")
```

Obviously the string could have been printed using:

```
print(name)
```

but it was being used as an example of indexing individual components within the string. The characters do not need to be indexed explicitly in Python; the loop variable can be assigned the value of each component:

```
for i in name:
    print (i, end="")
```

In this case the value of **i** is the value of the component, not its index. Each component of the string is assigned to **i** in turn, and there is no need to test for the end of the string or to know its length. This is a better way to access components in a string and, as it happens, can be used with all sequence types. Whether an index is used or the components are pulled out one at a time depends on the problem being solved; sometimes the index is needed, and other times it is not.

The Type *Bytes*

The type *bytes* represents a sequence of integers, albeit small ones. A *bytes* object of length 1 is an 8-bit integer, or a value between 0 and 255. A *bytes* object of length greater than 1 is a sequence of small integers. To be clear, if **s** is a *string* and **b** is a *bytes* then:

> **s[i]** is a character
>
> **b[i]** is a small integer

A *string* constant (literal) is a sequence of characters enclosed in quotes. A *bytes* literal is a sequence of characters enclosed in quotes and preceded by the letter 'b.' Thus:

```
'this is a string'
```

is a *string*, whereas:

```
b'this is a string'
```

has type *bytes*. Any method that applies to a *string* also applies to a *bytes* object, but bytes objects have some new ones. In particular, to convert a bytes object to a string, the **decode**() method is used, and a character encoding should be given as the parameter. If no parameter is given, then the decoding method is the one currently being used. There are a few possible decoding methods (e.g., "utf-8"). So to convert a bytes object **b** to a character string **s**, the following would work:

```
s = b.decode ("utf-8")
```

Questions remain: Why is the bytes type needed? What is it used for? Because (and this is a little ahead of what is needed) it implements the *buffer interface*. Certain file operations require a buffer interface to accomplish their tasks. Anything read from some specific types of file will be of the type *bytes*, for example, as it has that interface. This will be discussed further in future chapters, but for the moment it simply serves to explain why this sequence type exists at all. Other than the buffer interface, the bytes type is very much like a string, and can be converted back and forth.

Tuples

A *tuple* is almost identical to a string in basic structure, except that it is composed of arbitrary components instead of characters. The quotes can't be used to delimit a tuple because a string can be a component, so a tuple is generally enclosed in parentheses. The following are tuples:

```
tup1 = (2,3,5, 7, 11, 13, 17, 19)  # Prime numbers under 20
tup2 = ("Hydrogen","Helium","Lithium","Beryllium",
        "Boron","Carbon")
tup3 = "hi", "ohio", "salut"
```

If there is only one element in a tuple, there should be a comma at the end:

```
tup4 = ("one",)
tup5 = "two",
```

That's because it would not be possible otherwise to tell the difference between a tuple and a string enclosed in parentheses. Is (1) a tuple? Or is it simply the number 1?

A tuple can be empty:

```
tup = ()
```

Because they are like strings, each element in a tuple has an index, and they begin at 0. Tuples can be indexed and sliced, just like strings. So:

```
tup1[2:4] is (5, 7)
```

Concatenation is like that of strings too:

```
tup4 = tup4 + tup5     # yields tup4 = ('one', 'two')
```

As is the case with strings, the index -1 gives the last value in the tuple, -2 gives the second last, and so on. So in the example above, **tup2[-1]** is "Carbon." Also, like strings, the tuple type is immutable; this means that elements in the tuple can't be altered. Thus, statements such as:

```
tup1[2] = 6
tup3[1:] "bonjour"
```

are not allowed and will generate an error.

Tuples are an intermediate form between *strings*, which have just been discussed, and *lists*, which will be discussed next. They are simpler to implement than *list* (are *lightweight*) and are more general than strings.

Tuples underlie other aspects of Python.

Tuples in For Loops

Sequences can be used in a **for** loop to control the iteration and assign to the loop control variable. Tuples are interesting in this context because they can consist of strings, integers, or floats. The loop:

```
for i in ("Hydrogen","Helium","Lithium","Beryllium",
        "Boron","Carbon"):
```

will iterate six times, and the variable **i** will take on the values in the tuple in the order specified. The variable **i** is a string in this case. In cases where the types in the tuple are mixed, things are more complicated.

Problem: Print the Number of Neutrons in an Atomic Nucleus

Consider the tuple:

```
atoms=("Hydrogen",1,"Helium",2,"Lithium",3,
    "Beryllium",4,"Boron",5,"Carbon",6)
```

and the loop

```
for i in atoms:
    print (i)
```

This prints:

```
Hydrogen
1
Helium
2
Lithium
3
Beryllium
4
Boron
5
Carbon
6
```

The number following the name of the element is the atomic number of that element, the number of protons in the nucleus. In this case the type of the variable **i** alternates between string and integer. For elements with a low atomic number (less than 21), a good guess for the number of neutrons in the nucleus is twice the number of protons. The complexity is that some of the components are strings and some are integers. The program should only do the calculation when it is in an iteration having an integer value for the loop variable, because a string can't be multiplied by two.

A built-in function that can be of assistance is **isinstance**. It takes a variable and a type name and returns **True** if the variable is of that type and **False** otherwise. Using this function, here is a first stab at a program that makes the neutron guess:

```
atoms=("Hydrogen",1,"Helium",2,"Lithium",3,
    "Beryllium",4,"Boron",5,"Carbon",6)
for i in atoms:
    if isinstance(i, int):  # Is i an integer?
        j = i*2
        print ("has ", i, "protons and ", j, " neutrons.")
    else:
        print ("Element ", i)
```

In other words, in iterations where **i** is an integer as determined by **isinstance**, then **i** can legally be multiplied by 2 and the guess about number of neutrons can be printed.

Another way to solve the same problem would be to index the elements of the tuple. Elements 0,2,4, and so on (even indices) refer to element names, while the others refer to atomic numbers. This code would look as follows:

```
atoms=("Hydrogen",1,"Helium",2,"Lithium",3,
"Beryllium",4,"Boron",5,"Carbon",6)
```

```
for i in range(0,len(atoms)):
    if i%2 == 1:
        j = atoms[i]*2
        print ("has ", atoms[i], "protons and ",
               j, " neutrons.")
    else:
        print ("Element ", atoms[i])
```

Note that in this case the loop variable is always integer, and is not an element of the tuple but is an index at which to find an element. That's why the expression **atoms[i]** is used inside the loop instead of simply **i** as before.

Membership

Tuples are not sets in the mathematical sense, because an element can belong to a tuple more than once, and there is an order to the elements. However, some set operations could be implemented using tuples by looking at individual elements: set union and intersection, for example. The *intersection* of two sets A and B is the set of elements that are members of A and also members of B. The membership operator for tuples is the key word **in**:

```
if 1 in tuple1:       # 1 is an entry in tuple1
```

The intersection of A and B, where A and B are tuples, could be found using the following code:

```
for i in A:
    if i in B:
        C = C + i
```

The tuple C will be the intersection of A and B. It works by taking each known element of A and testing to see if it is a member of B; if so, it is added to C.

Problem: What Even Numbers Less than or Equal to 100 Are Also Perfect Squares?

This could be expressed as a set intersection problem. The set of even numbers less than 100 could be enumerated (this is not actual code):

A = (2,4,6,8,10 . . . and so on

or could be generated within a loop:

```
A = ()                    # Start with an empty tuple
for i in range(0,51):     # for appropriate integers
```

```
A = A + (i*2,)          # add the next even number to the
                          tuple
# Can't simply use A+i because i is integer, not a tuple.
```

Similarly, the perfect squares could be enumerated:

```
B = (4,9,16,25,36,49,64,81,100)
```

Or, again, created in a loop:

```
B = ()
for i in range(0,11):
    B = B + ((i*i),)
```

Now the set A can be examined, element by element, to see which members also belong to B:

```
C = ()
for i in A:
    if i in B:
        C = C + (i,)
```

The result is: (0, 4, 16, 36, 64, 100).

Two important things are learned from this. First, when constructing a new tuple from components, one can begin with an empty tuple. Second, individual components can be added to a tuple using the concatenation operator "+," but the element should be made into a tuple with one component before doing the concatenation.

Delete

A tuple is *immutable*, meaning that it cannot be altered. Individual elements can be indexed but not changed or deleted. What can be done to create a new tuple that has new elements; in particular, deleting an element means creating a new tuple that has all of the other elements except the one being deleted.

Problem: Delete the Element Lithium from the Tuple *atoms*, along with Its Atomic Number

Going back to the tuple **atoms**, deleting one of the components—in particular, *Lithium*—begins with determining which component *Lithium* is; that is, what is its index? So start at the first element of the tuple and look for the string "Lithium," stopping when it is found.

```
for i in range(0, len(atoms)):
    if atoms[i] == "Lithium":          # Found it at location i
        break;
else:
    i = -1                             # not found
```

Knowing the index of the element to be deleted, it is also known that all elements before that one belong to the new tuple and all elements after it do too. The elements before element **i** can be written as **atoms[0:i]**. Each element consists of a string and an integer, and assuming that both are to be deleted means that the elements following element **i** are **atoms[i+2:]**. In general to delete one element the second half would be **atoms[i+1:]**. Finishing the code that deletes "Lithium":

```
if i>=0:
    atoms = atoms[0:i] + atoms[i+2:]
```

So the tuple **atoms** has not been altered so much as it has been replaced completely with a new tuple that has no *Lithium* component.

Update

Again, because a tuple is *immutable* individual elements cannot be changed. A new tuple can created that has new elements; in particular, updating an element means creating a new tuple that has all of the other elements except the one being updated, and that includes the new value in the correct position.

Problem: Change the Entry for *Lithium* to an Entry for *Oxygen*

An update is usually a deletion followed by the insertion or addition of a new component. A deletion was done in the previous section, so what remains is to add a new component where the old one was deleted. Inserting the element *Oxygen* in place of *Lithium* would begin in the same way as the simple deletion already implemented:

```
for i in range(0, len(atoms)):
    if atoms[i] == "Lithium":          # Found it at location i
        break;
else:
    i = -1                             # not found
```

Next, a new tuple for Oxygen is created:

```
newtuple = ("Oxygen", 8)
```

Finally, this new tuple is placed at location **i**, while *Lithium* is removed:

```
if i>=0:
    atoms = atoms[0:i] + newtuple + atoms[i+2:]
```

However, an update may not always involve a deletion. If *Lithium* is not a component of the tuple **atoms**, then perhaps *Oxygen* should be added to **atoms** anyway. Where? How about at the end?

```
else:      # If i is -1 then the new tuple goes at the end
    atoms = atoms + newtuple
```

Tuple Assignment

One of the unique aspects of Python is so-called *tuple assignment*. When a tuple is assigned to a variable, the components are converted into an internal form that is the one tuples always use. This is called tuple packing, and it has already been encountered:

```
atoms=("Hydrogen",1,"Helium",2,"Lithium",3,
    "Beryllium",4,"Boron",5,"Carbon",6)
```

What is really interesting is that tuple *unpacking* can also be used. Consider the tuple:

```
srec = ('Parker', 'Jim', 1980, 'Math 550', 'C+', 'Cpsc 302', 'A+')
```

which is a tuple packing of a student record. It can be unpacked into individual variables in the following way:

```
(fname, lname, year, cmin, gmin, cmax, gmax) = srec
```

Which is the same as:

```
fname = srec[0]
lname = srec[1]
year  = srec[2]
cmin  = srec[4]
gmin  = srec[5]
cmax  = srec[6]
gmax  = srec[7]
```

Of course, the implication is that N variables can be assigned the value of N expressions or variables "simultaneously" if both are written as tuples. Examples would be:

```
(a, b, c, d, e) = (1,2,3,4,5)
(f, g, h, i, j) = (a, b, c, d, e)
```

The expression

```
(f, g, h, i, j) = 2 ** (a,b,c,d,e)
```

is *invalid* because the left side of "**" is not a tuple, and Python won't convert 2 into a tuple. Also:

```
(f, g, h, i, j) = (2,2,2,2,2) ** (a,b,c,d,e)
```

is also invalid because "**" is not defined on tuples, nor are other arithmetic operations. As with strings "+" means concatenation, though, so (1,2,3) + (4,5,6) yields (1,2,3,4,5,6).

Exchanging values between two variables is a common thing to do. It's an essential part of a sorting program, for example. The exchange in many languages requires three statements: a temporary copy of one of the variables has to be made during the swap:

```
temp = a
a = b
b = temp
```

Because of the way that tuples are implemented, this can be performed in one tuple assignment:

```
(a,b) = (b,a)
```

This is a little obscure—not to an experienced Python programmer, but certainly to a beginner. A Java programmer could see what was meant, but initially the rationale would not be obvious. This statement deserves a comment such as "perform an exchange of values using a tuple assignment."

Built-In Functions for Tuples

As examples for the table below, use the following:

```
T1 = (1,2,3,4,5)
T2 = (-1,2,4,5,7)
```

> **len**(T1) – Gives the number of components that are members of T1.
>
> **max**(T1) – Returns the largest element that is a component of T1.
>
> **min**(T1) – Returns the smallest element that is a component of T1.

In addition, tuples can be compared using the same operators as for integers and strings. Comparison is done on an element-by-element basis, just as it is with strings. In the example above **T1>T2** because at the first location where the two tuples differ (the initial component), the element in **T1** is greater than the corresponding element in **T2**. It is necessary for the corresponding elements of the tuple to be comparable; that is, they need to be of the same type. So if the tuples **t1** and **t2** are defined as:

```
t1 = (1, 2, 3, "4", "5")
t2 = (-1,2,4,5,7)
```

then the expression **t1>t2** is not allowed. A string can't be compared against an integer, and element 3 of **t1** is a string, whereas element 3 of **t2** is an int.

Lists

One way to think of a Python *list* is that it is a tuple in which the components can be modified. They have many properties of an *array* of the sort one might find in Java or C, in that they can be used as a place to store things and have random access to them; any element can be read or written. They are often used as one might use an array, but have a greater natural functionality.

Initially a list looks like a tuple, but uses square brackets.

```
list1=[2,3,5,7, 11, 13, 17, 19]  # Prime numbers under 20
list2=["Hydrogen","Helium","Lithium","Beryllium","Boron",
       "Carbon"]
list3=["hi", "ohio", "salut"]
```

A list can be empty:

```
list4 = []
```

and because they are like tuples and strings, each element in a list has an index, and they begin (as usual) at 0. Lists can be indexed and sliced, as before:

```
list1[2:4] is [5, 7]
```

Concatenation is like that of strings too:

```
list6 = list1 + [23, 31]
```

yields [2, 3, 5, 7, 11, 13, 17, 19, 23, 31]

Negative values index from the end of the string. However, unlike strings and tuples, individual elements can be modified. So:

```
list1[2] = 6
```

results in **list1** being [2, 3, 6, 7, 11, 13, 17, 19]. Also:

```
list3[1:] = "bonjour"
```

results in **list3** taking the value—*oops*, it becomes:

['hi', 'b', 'o', 'n', 'j', 'o', 'u', 'r'].

That's because a string is a sequence too, and this string consists of seven components. Each component of the string becomes a component of the list. If the string "bonjour" is supposed to become a single component of the list, then it needs to be done this way:

```
list3[1:] = ["bonjour"]
```

where the component is clearly defined as a list. The other components of **list3** are sequences, and now so is the new one. However, integers are *not* sequences, and the assignment:

```
list1[2] = [6,8,9]
```

results in the value of **list2** being:

```
[2, 3, [6, 8, 9], 7, 11, 13, 17, 19]
```

There is a list within this list; that is, the third component of **list1** is not an integer, but is a list of integers. That's legitimate, and works for tuples as well, but may not be what is intended.

Problem: Compute the Average (Mean) of a List of Numbers

The mean is the sum of all numbers in a collection divided by the number of numbers. If a set of numbers already exists as a list, calculating the mean might involve a loop that sums them followed by a division. For example, assuming that **list1** = [2, 3, 5, 7, 11, 13, 17, 19]:

```
mean = 0.0
for i in list1:
    mean = mean + i
mean = mean/len(list1)
```

It can be seen that a list can be used in a loop to define the values that the loop variable **i** will take on, a similar situation to that of a tuple. A second way to do the same thing would be:

```
mean = 0.0
for i in range(0,len(list1)):
    mean = mean + list1[i]
mean = mean/len(list1)
```

In this case the loop variable **i** is an index into the list and not a list element, but the result is the same. Python lists are more powerful than this, and making use of the extensive power of the list simplifies the calculation greatly:

```
mean = sum(list1) / len(list1)
```

The built-in function **sum** will calculate and return the sum of all of the elements in the list. That was the purpose of the loop, so the loop is not needed at all. The functions that work for tuples also work for lists (**min**, **max**, **len**), but some of the power of lists is in the methods a list provides.

Editing Lists

Editing a list means to change the values within it, usually to reflect a new situation to be handled by the program. The most obvious way to edit a list is to simply assign a new value to one of the components. For example:

```
list2 = ["Hydrogen","Helium","Lithium","Beryllium",
         "Boron","Carbon"]
list2[0] = "Nitrogen"
print (list2)
```

results in the following output:

['Nitrogen', 'Helium', 'Lithium', 'Beryllium', 'Boron', 'Carbon']

This substitution of a component is not possible with strings or tuples. It is possible to replace a single component with another list:

```
list2 = ["Hydrogen","Helium","Lithium","Beryllium",
         "Boron","Carbon"]
list2[0] = ["Hydrogen", "Nitrogen"]
```

results in:

```
list2 = [['Hydrogen','Nitrogen'],'Helium','Lithium',
         'Beryllium','Boron','Carbon']
```

Insert

To place new components within a list, the **insert** method is provided. This method places a component at a specified index; that is, the index of the new element will be the one given. To place "Nitrogen" at the beginning of list2, which is index 0:

```
list2.insert(0, "Nitrogen")
```

The first value given to **insert**, 0 in this case, is the index at which to place the component, and the second value is the thing to be inserted. Inserting "Nitrogen" at the end of the list would be accomplished by:

```
list2.insert(len(list2), "Nitrogen")
```

However, consider this:

```
list2.insert(-1, "Nitrogen")
```

Will this insert "Nitrogen" at the end? No. At the beginning of the statement, the value of **list2[-1]** is "Carbon." This is the value at index 5. Therefore, the insertion of "Nitrogen" will be at index 5, resulting in:

['Hydrogen', 'Helium', 'Lithium', 'Beryllium', 'Boron', 'Nitrogen', 'Carbon']

Append

A way to add something to the end of a list is to use the **append** method:

```
list2.append("Nitrogen")
```

results in:

['Hydrogen', 'Helium', 'Lithium', 'Beryllium', 'Boron', 'Carbon', 'Nitrogen']

Remember, the "+" operation will only concatenate a list to a list, so the equivalent expression involving "+" would be:

```
list2 = list2 + ["Nitrogen"]
```

Extend

The **extend** method does pretty much the same things as the "+" operator. With the definitions:

```
a = [1,2,3,4,5]
b = [6,7,8,9,10]
print (a+b)
a.extend(b)
print(a)
```

the output is:

[1, 2, 3, 4, 5, 6, 7, 8, 9, 10]
[1, 2, 3, 4, 5, 6, 7, 8, 9, 10]

However, if **append** had been used instead of **extend**:

```
a = [1,2,3,4,5]
b = [6,7,8,9,10]
print (a+b)
a.append(b)
print(a)
```

the result would have been:

[1, 2, 3, 4, 5, 6, 7, 8, 9, 10]
[1, 2, 3, 4, 5, [6, 7, 8, 9, 10]]

Remove

The remove method does what is expected: it removes an element from the list. But unlike insert, for example, it does not do it using an index; the value to be removed is specified. So:

```
list1 = ["Hydrogen","Helium","Lithium",
        "Beryllium","Boron","Carbon"]
list1.remove("Helium")
```

results in the **list1** being ['Hydrogen', 'Lithium', 'Beryllium', 'Boron', 'Carbon']. Unfortunately, if the component being deleted is not a member of the list, then an error occurs. There are ways to deal with that, or a test can be made for trying to delete an item:

```
if "Nitrogen" in list1:
    list1.remove("Nitrogen")
```

If there is more than a single instance of the item being removed, then only the first one will be removed.

Index

When discussing *tuples* it was learned that the **index** method looked through the tuple and found the index at which a specified item occurred. The **index** method for lists works in the same way. So:

```
list1 = ["Hydrogen","Helium","Lithium",
         "Beryllium","Boron","Carbon"]
print (list1.index("Boron"))
```

prints "4," because the string "Boron" appears at index 4 in this list (starting from 0, of course). If there is more than one occurrence of "Boron" in the list, then the index of the first one (i.e., the smallest index) is returned. If the value is not found in the string, then an error occurs. Again, it might be appropriate to check:

```
if "Boron" in list1:
    print (list1.index("Boron"))
```

Sort

This method places the components of a list into ascending order. Using the **list1** variable that has been used so often:

```
list1 = ["Hydrogen","Helium","Lithium",
         "Beryllium","Boron","Carbon"]
list1.sort()
print(list1)
```

the result is:

['Beryllium', 'Boron', 'Carbon', 'Helium', 'Hydrogen', 'Lithium']

which is in alphabetical order. The method will sort integers and floating-point numbers as well. Strings and numbers cannot be mixed, though, because they can't be compared. So:

```
list2 = ["Hydrogen",1,"Helium",2,"Lithium",3,
         "Beryllium",4,"Boron",5]
list2.sort()
```

results in an error that will be something like

```
    list2.sort()
TypeError: unorderable types: int() < str()
```

The meaning of this error should be clear. Things of type **int** (*integer*) and things of type **str** (*string*) can't be compared against each other and so can't be placed in a sensible order if mixed. For sort to work properly, all of the elements of the list must be of the same type. It is always possible to convert one type of thing into another, and in Python converting an integer to a string is accomplished with the **str()** function; string to integer is converted using **int()**. So **str(3)** would result in "3," and **int("12")** is 12. An error will occur if it is not possible, so **int(12.2)** will fail.

If each element of a list is itself a list, it can still be sorted. Consider the list:

```
z = [["Hydrogen",3], ["Hydrogen",2], ["Lithium",3],
        ["Beryllium",4], ["Boron",5]]
```

When sorted this becomes:

```
[['Beryllium',4],['Boron',5],['Hydrogen',2],['Hydrogen',3],
['Lithium',3]]
```

Each component of this list is compatible with the others, consisting of a string and an integer. Thus, they can be compared against each other. Notice that there are two entries for hydrogen: one with a number 2 and one with a number 3. The **sort** method arranges them correctly. A list is sorted by individual elements in sequence order, so the first thing tested would be the string. If those are the same, then the next element is checked. That's an integer, so the component with the smallest integer component will come first.

Reverse

In any sequence the order of the components within it is important. Reversing that order is a logical operation to provide, but it may not be used very often. One instance where it can be important is after a sort. The **sort** method always places components into *ascending* order. If they are supposed to be in *descending* order, then the **reverse** method becomes valuable. As an example consider sorting the list **q**:

```
q = [5, 6, 1, 5, 4, 9, 9, 1, 6, 3]
q.sort()
```

The value of **q** at this point is

[1, 1, 3, 4, 5, 5, 6, 6, 9, 9]

To place this list is descending order the reverse method is used:

```
q.reverse()
```

and the result is

[9, 9, 6, 6, 5, 5, 4, 3, 1, 1]

Count

This method is used to determine how many times a potential component of a list actually occurs. It *does not return the number of elements in the list*—that job is done by the **len** function. Using the list **q** as an example:

```
q = [5, 6, 1, 5, 4, 9, 9, 1, 6, 3]
print (1,q.count(1), 2, q.count(2), 3,
            q.count(3), 99, q.count(99))
```

will result in the output:

      1 2   2 0   3 1   99 0

where the spacing is enhanced for emphasis. This says that there are 2 instances of the number 1 (1,2) in the list, zero instances of 2 (2,0), one instance of the number 3 (3,1) and none of 99 (99,0).

List Comprehension

When creating a list of items, two mechanisms have been discussed. The first is to use constants, as in the list **q** in the previous section. The second appends items to a list, and this could be done within a loop. Making a list of perfect squares could be done like this:

```
t = []
for i in range(0,10):
    t = t + [i*i]
```

which creates the list [0, 1, 4, 9, 16, 25, 36, 49, 64, 81]. This kind of thing is common enough that a special syntax has been created for it in Python—the *list comprehension*.

The basic idea is simple enough, although some specific cases are complicated. In the previous situation involving perfect squares, the elements in the list are some function of the index. When that is true the loop, index, and function can be given within the square brackets as a definition of the list. So, the list **t** could be defined as:

```
tt = [i**2 for i in range(10)]
```

The **for** loop is within the square brackets, indicating that the purpose is to define components of the list. The variable **i** here is the loop variable, and **i°°2** is the function that creates the elements from the index. This is a simple example of a list comprehension.

Creating random integer values? No problem:

```
tt = [random.randint(0,100) for i in range(10)]
```

The first six elements in all uppercase?

```
list1 = ["Hydrogen","Helium","Lithium","Beryllium",
        "Boron","Carbon"]
        ss = [i.upper() for i in list1]
```

This is a very effective way to create lists, but it does depend on having a known connection between the index and the element.

Lists and Tuples

A tuple can be converted into a list. Lists have a greater functionality than tuples; that is, they provide more operations and a greater ability to represent data. On the other hand, they are more complicated and require more computer resources. If something can be represented as a tuple, then it is likely best to do so. A tuple is designed to be a collection of elements that as a whole represent some more complicated object, but that individually are perhaps of different types. This is rather like a C *struct* or Pascal *record*. A list is more often used to hold a set of elements that all have the same type, more like an array. This is a good way to think of the two types when deciding what to use to solve a specific problem.

Python provides tools for conversion. The built-in function **list** takes a tuple and converts it into a list; the function tuple does the reverse, taking a list and turning it into a tuple. For example, converting list1 into a tuple:

```
tuple1 = tuple(list1)
print(tuple1)
```

yields

('Hydrogen', 'Helium', 'Lithium', 'Beryllium', 'Boron', 'Carbon')

This is seen to be a tuple because of the '(' and ')' delimiters. The reverse:

```
v = list(tuple1)
print(v)
```

prints the text line:

['Hydrogen', 'Helium', 'Lithium', 'Beryllium', 'Boron', 'Carbon']

and the square brackets indicate this is a list.

Exceptions

Exceptions are the usual way to check for errors of indexing and membership in lists. The error is allowed to occur, but an exception is tested and handled in the case where, for example, an item being deleted is not in the list.

Problem: Delete a Specified Element from a List

Given the same list, read an element from the keyboard and delete that element from the list. The basic code is the same, but now the string is entered and could be anything at all. It's easier to test a program when it can be made to fail on purpose. The name is entered using the **input** function and is used as the parameter to **remove**. Now it is possible to test all of the code in this program without changing it. First, here is the program:

```
list1 = ["Hydrogen","Helium","Lithium","Beryllium",
        "Boron","Carbon"]
s = input("Enter:")
try:
    list1.remove(s)
except:
    print ('Can't find ', s)
print (list1)
```

Properly testing a program means executing all of the statements that comprise it and ensuring that the answer given is correct. So in this case, first delete an element that is a part of the list. Try Lithium. Here is the output:

Enter: Lithium

['Hydrogen', 'Helium', 'Beryllium', 'Boron', 'Carbon']

This is correct. These are the statements that were executed in this instance:

```
list1 = ["Hydrogen","Helium","Lithium","Beryllium",
        "Boron","Carbon"]
```

```
s = input("Enter:")
try:
    list1.remove(s)   # This was successful
print (list1)
```

Now try to delete *Oxygen*. Output is:

> Enter: Oxygen
>
> Can't find Oxygen
>
> ['Hydrogen', 'Helium', 'Lithium', 'Beryllium', 'Boron', 'Carbon']

This is correct. These statements were executed:

```
list1 = ["Hydrogen","Helium","Lithium","Beryllium",
        "Boron","Carbon"]
s = input("Enter:")
try:
    list1.remove(s)     # this was not successful
except:
    print ('Can't find ', s)
print (list1)
```

All of the code in the program has been executed and the results checked for both major situations. For any major piece of software, this kind of testing is exhausting, but it is really the only way to minimize the errors that remain in the final program.

Set Types

Something of type *set* is an unordered collection of objects. An element can only be a member of a given *set* once, so in that sense it is much like a mathematical set. In fact, that's the point. Because a set is unordered, operations such as indexing and slicing are not provided. It does support membership (**is**), size (**len()**), and looping on membership (**for i in set**).

Anyone (probably an older person) who knows the *Pascal* language has some familiarity with the set type in Python.

Mathematical sets have certain specific, well-defined operations, and those are available on a Python set also.

Subset	**set1 < set2** means **set1** is a true subset of **s2**.
Intersection	**set1 & set2** creates a new set containing members in common with both.

Union	**set1	set2** creates a new set with all elements of both.
Difference	**set1-set2** creates a new set with members that are not in both.
Equality	**set1==set2** is true if both sets contain only the same elements.

Creating a new object of type *set* is a matter of specifying either that it is a *set* or what the elements are. So, one way is to use the {} syntax:

```
set1 = {1,3,5,7,9}
```

or to use the constructor:

```
set2 = set(range(1, 10))
```

which gives the set {1, 2, 3, 4, 5, 6, 7, 8, 9}. So:

> **set1<set2** is True
> **set1 & set2** is {9, 1, 3, 5, 7}   Note: order does not matter to a set.
> **set1 | set2** is {1, 2, 3, 4, 5, 6, 7, 8, 9}
> **set2 − set1** is {8, 2, 4, 6}

A new element can be added to a set using **add()**:

```
set1.add(11)
```

and removed using **remove()**:

```
set1.remove(11)
```

or **discard()**:

```
set1.discard(11)
```

If the element being removed is not in the set, then an error will occur (*KeyError*) when **remove()** is called, but not with **discard()**. This should be tested first or be placed in an **except** statement.

All of the examples so far involve integers belonging to a set, but other types can belong as well: floating-point numbers, strings, and even tuples (not *lists*). For example, the following are legal sets:

```
{"a", "e", "i", "o", "u"}
{"cyan", "yellow", "magenta"}
{ (2,4), (3,9), (4,16), (5,25), (6,36), (7,49) }
```

Example: Craps

Craps is a dice game, for those unfamiliar with it, and commonly involves betting on the outcome. The player (*shooter*) rolls two dice. If, on the first roll (*pass*), a total of 7 or 11 is obtained, then the shooter wins. On the other hand, an initial roll of 2, 3, or 12 loses immediately. Any other roll is called the *point*. In that case the shooter continues to roll the dice. If a 7 is obtained then the shooter loses, and if the point number is rolled then the shooter wins. The shooter continues to roll until one or the other occurs. One way to implement this game in Python is to use sets.

Elements of the sets will be values on each die, which is to say one roll. There are two dice so a total of 36 combinations exist. A single roll is a tuple, such as (1,1) or (3,4). There are only 12 distinct sums of two dice, and multiple ways to achieve them. A sequence named **roll** will be created that contains a set for each possible value, and that set contains all of the ways that the value can be obtained. For instance, there are two ways to roll a 3, so:

roll[3] = {(1,2), (2,1)}

Initially a set is created for each possible roll of a pair of dice and then is initialized as described:

```
from random import *

roll = list(range(0,13))      # Create the empty list
for i in range(1,13):         # and fill with empty sets.
    roll[i] = set()

for i in range (1,7):         # Now for each possible roll
    for j in range (1,7):     # of two dice, add that roll
        k = i+j               # to the element of roll for
        roll[k].add( (i,j) )  # that value (sum of the dice)
```

Now **roll[i]** contains all of the ways to roll a value of **i**. In particular, **roll[7]** contains all ways to roll a 7 and **roll[11]** contains all ways to roll an 11. Thus, all of the rolls that will win on the first pass can be placed in a single set, the union of **roll[7]** and **roll[11]**:

```
winner = roll[7] | roll[11]
```

Similarly the rolls that will lose for the shooter on the first pass are:

```
loser = roll[2] | roll[3] | roll[12]
```

If any other roll is thrown, then that becomes the point. Rolling a die amounts to getting a random number between 1 and 6 inclusive, or:

```
die1 = randrange(1,7)
die2 = randrange(1,7)
```

Remember that **randrange()** produces a number *less* than the second parameter. Given this roll, the point is the set **roll[die1+die2]**. Continuing the program from the die rolls:

```
val = (die1,die2)              # A tuple, the current roll
print ("Shooter rolls ", val)
if val in winner:              # Is this tuple a winner?
    print ("The shooter wins!")
elif val in loser:            # Is it a loser?
    print ("The shooter loses")
else:
    point = roll[die1+die2]    # Define the point set
    print (die1+die2, " is your point.")
```

Now the dice are rolled repeatedly. If the roll is in the point set, then the shooter wins. If the roll is a 7 (in the set **roll[7]**) then the player loses. Otherwise the shooter rolls again.

```
while True:                  # Repeat until a win or loss happens
    die1 = randrange(1,7)    # Roll the dice
    die2 = randrange(1,7)
    val = (die1, die2)       # val is a tuple
    print ("Rolls ", val)
    if val in roll[7]:       # Any 7 roll loses
        print ("The shooter loses!")
        break
    if val in point:         # Rolling the 'point' wins.
        print ("The shooter makes the point. A winner!")
        break
```

In a real craps game this entire process is repeated, and bets are placed.

4

FUNCTIONS

U nlike in the cases of **if** statements or **for** statements, a function definition in Python does not involve the word 'function.' As an example of a simple definition, imagine a program that needs a function to print twenty "#" characters on a line. It could be defined as:

```
def pound20 ():
    for i in range (0,20):
        print ("#", end="")
```

The word **def** is known to Python and always begins the definition of a function. This is followed by the name of the function, in this case **pound20** because the function prints 20 *pound* characters ("#"). Then comes the list of parameters, which can be thought of as a tuple of variable names. In this case the tuple is empty, meaning that nothing is passed to the function. Finally comes the ":" character that defines a new suite that comprises the code belonging to the function. From here on the code is indented one more level, and when the indentation reverts to the original level, the function definition is complete.

Calling this function is a matter of using its name as a statement or in an expression, being careful to always include the tuple of parameters. Even when the tuple is empty it helps distinguish a function from a variable. A call to this function would be:

```
pound20 ()
```

and the result would be that 20 "#" characters would be printed on one line of the output console.

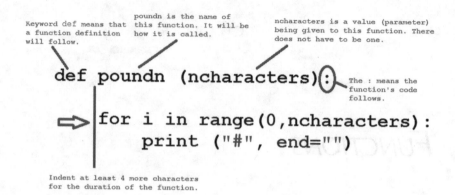

Keyword def means that a function definition will follow.

poundn is the name of this function. It will be how it is called.

ncharacters is a value (parameter) being given to this function. There does not have to be one.

The : means the function's code follows.

Indent at least 4 more characters for the duration of the function.

FIGURE 4.1. The syntax of a function definition.

A function can be *passed* one or more values that will determine the result of the function. A function **cosine**, for example, would be passed an angle, and that angle would be used to compute the cosine. Each call to **cosine** passing a different value can yield a different result. In the case of the function that prints pound characters, it might be useful to pass it the number of pound characters to print. It should not be called **pound20** anymore, because it does not always print 20 characters. It will be called **poundn** this time:

```
def poundn (ncharacters):
    for i in range(0,ncharacters):
        print ("#", end="")
```

The variable **ncharacters** that is given in parentheses after the function name is called a *parameter* or an *argument*, and indicates the name by which the function will refer to the value passed to it. This name is known only inside of the function, and while it can be modified within the function, this modification will not have any bearing on anything outside. The call to **poundn** must now include a value to be passed to the function:

```
poundn (3)
```

When this call is performed the code within **poundn** begins executing, and the value of **ncharacters** is 3, the value that was passed. It prints 3 characters and returns. A subsequent call to **poundn** could be passed a different number, perhaps 8, and then **ncharacters** would take on the value 8 and the function would print 8 characters. It will print as many characters as requested through the parameter.

NOTE A **def** statement is not a declaration. Such things are foreign to Python. A **def** statement executes, and it effectively "creates" a new function each time it is executed.

Function Execution

All functions return a value, and as such can be treated within expressions as if they were variables. They cannot be assigned to, but otherwise have the same utility. So, assuming the existence of a cosine function, it could be used in an expression in the usual ways. For example:

```
x = cosine(x)*r
while cosine(x) < 0.5:
print (cosine(x)*cosine(x))
```

In these cases the value returned by the function is used by the code to calculate a further value or to create output. The expression "cosine(x)" resolves to a value of some Python type. The most common purpose of a function is to calculate a value, which is then returned to the calling part of the program and will possibly be used in a further calculation.

The **return** statement assigns a value and a type to the object returned by the function. It also stops executing the function and resumes execution at the location where the function was called. A simple example would be to return a single value, such as an integer or floating-point number:

```
return 0
```

returns the value 0 from a function. The return value could be an expression:

```
return x*x + y*y
```

A function has only one return value, but it can be of any type, so it could be a list or tuple that contains multiple components:

```
return (2,3,5,7,11)
return ["fluorine","chlorine","bromine","iodine"]
```

Expressions can include function calls, so a return value can be defined in this way as well; for example

```
return cosine(x)
```

One of the simplest functions that can be used as an example is one that calculates the square of its parameter. It nonetheless illustrates some interesting things:

```
def square (x):
    return x*x
```

The print statement:

```
print (square(12))
```

will print:

```
144
```

Interestingly, the statement:

```
print(square(12.0))
```

results in:

```
144.0
```

The same function returns an integer in one case and a float in the other. Why? Because the function returns the result of an expression involving its parameter, which in one case was integer and in the other was real. This implies that a function has no fixed type, and can return any type at all. Indeed, the same function can have return statements that return an integer, a float, a string, and a list independent of type of the parameter passed:

```
def test (x):   # Return one of four types depending on x
    if x<1:
        return 1
    if x<2:
        return 2.0
    if x<3:
        return "3"
    return [1,2,3,4]

print (test(0))
print (test(1))
print (test(2))
print (test(3))
```

The output:

```
1
2.0
3
[1, 2, 3, 4]
```

Problem: Write a Function to Calculate the Square Root of Its Parameter

Two thousand years ago the Babylonians had a way to calculate the square root of a number. They understood the definition of a square root: that if $y*y = x$ then y is the square root of x. They figured out that if y was an overestimate to the true value of the square root of x, then x/y would be an underestimate. In that case, a better guess would be to average those two values: the next guess would be $y1 = (y + x/y)/2$. The guess after that would be $y2 = (y1+x/y1)/2$, and so on. At any point in the calculation the error (difference between the correct answer and the estimate) can be found by squaring the guess yi and subtracting x from it, knowing that $yi*yi$ is supposed to equal x.

The function will therefore start by guessing what the square root might be. It cannot be 0 because then x/y would be undefined. x is a good guess. Then construct a loop based on the expression $y2 = (y1+x/y1)/2$, or more generally $yi+1 = (yi+x/yi)/2$ for iteration i. At first, run this loop a fixed number of times, perhaps 20. Here is the function that results:

```
def root (x):            # Compute the square root of x
    y = x                # First guess: too big, probably
    for i in range(1, 20):   # Iterate20 times
        y = (y + x/y)/2.0    # Average the prior guess and x/y
    return y             # Return the last guess
```

This correctly computes the square root of 2 to 15 decimal places. This is probably more than is necessary, meaning that the loop is executing more times than it needs to. In fact, changing the 20 iterations to only 6 still gives 15 correct places. This is exceptional accuracy: if the distance between the Earth and the Sun were known this accurately it would be within 0.006 inches of the correct value. The Babylonians seem to have been very clever.

What's the square root of 10000? If the number of iterations is kept at 6, then the answer is a very poor one indeed: 323.1. Why? Some numbers (large ones) need more iterations than others. To guarantee that a good estimate of the square root is returned, an estimate of the error should be used. When the error is small enough, then the value will be good enough. The error will be $x-yi*yi$. The function should not loop a fixed number of times, but instead should repeat until the error is less than, say, 0.0000001. This function will be named **roote**, where the "e" is for "error."

```
# Computer the square root of X to 7 decimal places
def roote (x):
    y = x                # y is supposed to be the square root of x, so
```

```
e = abs(x-y*y)          # the error is x - y*y
while e > 0.0000001:    # repeat while the error is bigger
                        # than 0.0000001
    y = (y + x/y)/2.0   # New estimate for square root
    e = abs(x-y*y)      New error value
return y
```

This function will return the square root of any positive value of **x** to within 7 decimal places. It should check for negative values, though.

Parameters

A parameter can be either a name, meaning that it is a Python *variable* (object) of some kind, or an *expression*, meaning it has a value but no permanence in that it can't be accessed later on—it has no name. Both are passed to a function as an *object reference*. The expression is evaluated before being given to the function and its type does not matter in so far as Python will always know what it is; its value is assigned a name when it is passed. Consider, for example, the function **square** in the following context:

```
...
pi = 3.14159
r = 2.54
c = square (2*pi*r)
print ("Circumference is ", c)
```

The assignments to **pi** and **r** are performed, and when the call to **square** occurs, the expression **2*pi*r** is evaluated first. Its value is assigned to a temporary variable, which is passed as the parameter to square. Inside the function this parameter is named **x**, and the function calculates x squared and returns it as a value. It is as if the following code executes:

```
pi = 3.14159
r = 2.54
# call square(2*pi*r)
 parameter1 = 2*pi*r   # set the parameter value
 x = parameter1 # First parameter is named x inside SQUARE
 returnvalue = x*x     # Code within SQUARE, return x*x
c = returnvalue   # assign result of function call to c
print ("Circumference is ", c)
```

This is not how a function is implemented, but shows how the parameter is effectively passed; a copy is made of the parameters and those are passed. If the expression **2*pi*r** was changed to a simple variable, then the internal location of that variable would be passed.

Passing more structured objects works the same way but can behave differently. If a list is passed to a function, then the list itself cannot be modified, but the contents of the list can be. The list is assigned another name, but it is the same list. To be clear, consider a simple function that edits a list by adding a new element to the end:

```
def addend  (arg):
    arg.append("End")

z = ["Start", "Add", "Multiply"]
print (1, z)
addend(z)
print (1, z)
```

The list associated with the variable z is changed by this function call. It now ends with the string "End." Output from this is:

> 1 ['Start', 'Add', 'Multiply']
> 2 ['Start', 'Add', 'Multiply', 'End']

Why is this? Because the name **z** refers to a thing that consists of many other parts. The name **z** is used to access them, and the function can't modify the value of z itself. It *can* modify what **z** indicates; that is, the components. Think of it, if it makes it simpler, as a level of indirection. A book can be exchanged between two people. The receiver writes a note in it and gives it back. It's the same book, but the contents are now different.

A small modification to **addend()** illustrates some confusing behavior. Instead of using **append** to add "End" to the list, use the concatenation operator "+":

```
def addend (arg):
    arg = arg + ["End"]

z = ["Start", "Add", "Multiply"]
print (1, z)
addend(z)
print (2, z)
```

Now the output is:

> 1 ['Start', 'Add', 'Multiply']
> 2 ['Start', 'Add', 'Multiply']

The component "End" is not a part of the list **z** anymore. It was made a component inside of the function, but it's not present after the function returns. This is because the statement:

```
arg = arg + ["End"]
```

actually creates a new list with "End" as the final component, and then assigns that new list as a value to **arg**. This represents an attempt to change the value that was passed, which can't happen: changing the value of **arg** will not change the value of the passed variable **z**. So, within the function **arg** is a new list with "End" as the final component. Outside, the list **z** has not changed.

The way that Python passes parameters is the subject of a lot of discussion on Internet blogs and lists. There are many names given for the method used, and while the technique is understood, it does differ from the way parameters are passed in other languages and is confusing to people who learned another language like Java or C before Python. The thing to remember is that the actual value of the thing (an *object reference*) being passed can't be assigned a new value inside the function, but the things that it *references* or *points to* can be modified.

Default Parameters

It is possible to specify a value for a parameter in the instance that it is not given one by the caller. That may not seem to make sense, but the implication is that it will sometimes be passed explicitly and sometimes not. When debugging code it is common to embed **print** statements in specific places to show that the program has reached that point. Sometimes it is important to print out a variable or value there, other times it's just to indicate that the program got to that statement safely. Consider a function named **gothere**:

```
def gothere (count, value):
    print ("Got Here: ",count, " value is ", value)
```

then throughout the program, calls to **gothere** would be sprinkled with a different value for **count** every time; the value of **count** indicates the statement that has been reached. This is a way of *instrumenting* the program, and can be very useful for finding errors. So the code being debugged may look like:

```
year = 2015    # The code below is not especially meaningful
a = year % 19  # and is an example only.
gothere(1, 0)
b = year // 100
c = year % 100
gothere (2, 0)
d = (19*a+b-b//4-((b-(b + 8)//25 + 1)//3)+15)%30
```

```
e = (32+2 * (b % 4) + 2 * (c // 4) - d - (c % 4)) % 7
f = d + e - 7 * ((a + 11 * d + 22 * e) // 451) + 114
gothere (3, f)
month = f // 31
day = f % 31 + 1
gothere(4, day)
return date(year, month, day)
```

Output is:

```
Got Here: 1 value is 0
Got Here: 2 value is 0
Got Here: 3 value is 128
Got Here: 4 value is 5
2015 4 5
```

The program reaches each of the four checkpoints and prints a proper message. The first two calls to **gothere** did not need to print a value, only the count number. The second parameter could be given a default value, perhaps **None**, and then it would not have to be passed. The definition of the function would now be:

```
def gothere (count, value=None):
    if value:
        print ("Got Here: ",count, " value is ", value)
    else:
        print (Got Here: ", count)
```

and the output this time is:

```
Got Here: 1
Got Here: 2
Got Here: 3 value is 128
Got Here: 4 value is 5
2015 4 5
```

The assignment within the parameter list gives the name value a special property. It has a *default value*. If the parameter is not passed, then it takes that value; otherwise it behaves normally. This also means that **gothere** can be called with one or two parameters, which can be very handy. It is important to note that the parameters that are given a default value must be defined after the ones that are not. That's because otherwise it would not be clear what was being passed. Consider the (illegal) definition:

```
def wrong (a=1, b, c=12):
    . . .
```

Now call **wrong** with two parameters:

```
wrong (2,5)
```

What parameters are being passed? Is it **a** and **b**? Is it **a** and **c**? It is impossible to tell. A legal definition would be:

```
def right (b, a=1, c=12)
```

This function can be called as

```
right (19)
```

in which case b=19, a=1, and c=12. It can be called as:

```
right (19, 20)
```

in which case b=19, a=19, and c=12. It can be called as:

```
right (19, 19, 19)
```

in which case b=19, a=19, and c=19. But how can it be called passing **b** and **c** but not **a**? Like this:

```
right (19, c=19)
```

In this case **a** has been allowed to default. The only way to pass **c** without also passing **a** is to give its name explicitly so that the call is not ambiguous.

None

The value of the name None is something that has no value. It's like null or nil in other languages, but is more general. For example, a function that is not explicitly assigned a return value will return **None**.

None has its own type (*NoneType*), and is used to indicate something that has no defined value or the absence of a value. It can be explicitly assigned to variables, printed, returned from a function, and tested. Testing for this value can be done using:

```
if x == None:
```

or by:

```
if x is None:
```

Example: The Game of Sticks

This is a relatively simple combinatorial game that involves removing sticks or chips from a pile. There are two players, and the game begins with a pile of 21 sticks. The first player begins by removing 1, 2, or 3 sticks from the pile. Then the next player removes some sticks, again 1, 2, or 3 of them. Players alternate in this way. The player who removes the last stick wins the game; in other words, if you can't move, you lose.

Functions are useful in the implementation of this game because both players do similar things. The action connected with making a move, displaying the current position, and so on are the same for the human player and the computer opponent. The current status or state of the game is simply a number, the number of sticks remaining in the pile. When that number is zero then the game is over, and the loser is whatever player is supposed to move next. The code for a pair of moves, one from the human and one from the computer, might be coded in Python as follows:

```
displayState(val)                      # Show the game board
userMove = getMove()                   # Ask user for their move
val = val - userMove                   # Make the move
print ("You took ", userMove, " sticks leaving ", val)
if gameOver(val):
    print("You win!")
else:
    move = makeComputerMove (val)      # Calculate the
                                       computer's move
    print ("Computer took ", move, " sticks leaving ", val)
    if gameOver(val):
        print("Computer wins!")
```

The current state of the game is displayed first, and then the human player is asked for their move. The move is simply the number of sticks to remove. When the move has been made, if there are no sticks left then the human wins. Otherwise, the computer calculates and makes a move; again, if no sticks remain then the game is over, in this case the computer being the winner. This entire section of code needs to be repeated until the game is over, of course.

There are four functions that must be written for this version: **displayState()**, **getMove()**, **gameOver()**, and **makeComputerMove()**.

The function **displayState()** prints the current situation in the game. Specifically, it prints one 'O' character for each stick still in the pile, and does so in rows of 6. At the beginning of the game this function would print:

```
O O O O O O
O O O O O O
O O O O O O
O O O
```

which is 21 sticks. The code is:

```
def displayState(val):
    k = val          # K represents the number of sticks
                     not printed
    while k > 0:     # So long as some are not printed . . .
        if k >=6:    # If there is a whole row, print it.
            print ("O O O O O O ", end="")
            k = k - 6         # Six fewer sticks are unprinted
        else:
            for j in range(0,k):  # Print the remainder
                print ("O ", end="")
            k = 0                 # None remain
    print ("")
```

This should be obvious. Also note that the function is named for what it does, and it does only one thing; it modifies no values outside of the function, and it serves a purpose that is needed multiple times. These are all good properties of a function.

The function **getMove()** will print a prompt to the user/player asking for the number of sticks they wish to remove and reads that value from the keyboard, returning it as the function value. Again, this function is named for what it does and performs a single, simple task. One possibility for the code is:

```
def getMove ():
    n = int(input ("Your move: Take away how many?   "))
    while n<=0 or n>3:
        print ("Sorry, you must take 1, 2, or 3 sticks.")
        n = int(input ("Your move: Take away how many?   "))
    return n
```

The function **gameOver()** is trivial, but lends structure to the program. All it does is test to see whether the value of **val**, the game state variable, is zero. It leaves open the idea that there may be other end-of-game indicators that could be tested here.

```
def gameOver (state):
    if state == 0:
```

```
      return True
   return False
```

Finally, the most complicated function, **getComputerMove()**, can be attempted. Naturally a good game presents a challenge to the player, and so the computer should win the game it if can. It should not play randomly if that is possible. In the case of this particular game, the winning strategy is easy to code. The player to make the final move wins, so if there are 1, 2, or 3 sticks left at the end, the computer would take them all and win. Forcing the human player to have 4 sticks makes this happen. The same is true if the computer can give the human player (i.e., leave the game in the state having) 8, 12, or 16 sticks (Check this!). So, if the human moves first (as it does in this implementation), the computer tries to leave the game in a state where there are 16, 12, 8, or 4 sticks left after its move. The code could be:

```
def getComputerMove (val):
    n = val % 4
    if n<=0:
        return 1
    else:
        return n
```

There are a couple of details needed to finish this game properly that are left as an exercise.

Scope

A variable that is defined (first used) in the main program is called a *global* variable, and can be accessed by all functions if they ask for it. A variable that is used in a function can be accessed by that function, and is not available in the main program. It's called a *local* variable. This scheme is called *scoping*: the locations in a program where a variable can be accessed is called its *scope*. It's all pretty clear unless a global variable has the same name as a local one, in which case the question is: "What value is represented by this name?" If a variable named "x" is global and a function also declares a variable having the same name, this is called *aliasing*, and it can be a problem.

In Python a variable is assumed to be local unless the programmer specifically says it is global. This is done in a statement; for example:

```
global a, b, c
```

tells Python that the variables named **a**, **b**, and **c** are global variables and are defined outside of the function. This means that after the function has completed execution, those variables can still be accessed by the main program and by any other functions that declare them to be global.

Global variables are thought by some programmers to be a bad thing, but in fact they can be quite useful and can assist in the generality of the functions that are a part of the program. A global variable should represent something that is, in fact, global, something that should be known to the whole program. For instance, if the program is one that plays checkers or chess, then the board can be global. There is only one board, and it is essential to the whole program. The same applies to any program that has a central set of data that many of the functions need to modify.

An example of central data is game state in a video game. In the Sticks game program, for example, the function **getComputerMove**() takes a parameter—the game state. There is only one game state, and although for some games it can involve many values, in this case there is only one value: the number of sticks remaining. The function can be rewritten to use the game state variable **val** as a global in the following way:

```
def getComputerMove ():
    global val
    n = val % 4
    if n<=0:
        return 1
    else:
        return n
```

Similarly, the function that determines whether the game is over could use **val** as a global variable. On the other hand it would be poor stylistic form to have **getMove**() to use a global for the user's move. The name does imply that the function will get a move, and so that value should be returned as an explicit function return value.

If a variable is named as global then that name cannot be used in the function as a local variable as well. It would be impossible to access it and would be confusing. It is a common programming error to forget to declare a variable as global. When this happens the variable is a new one local to the function, and starts out with a value of 0. Thus no syntax error is detected, but the calculation will almost certainly be incorrect. It might be a good idea to identify global variables in their name. For example, place the string "_g" at the end of the names of all globals. The game state above would be named **val_g** for example. This will be a reminder to declare them properly within functions.

Other kinds of data that could be kept globally would include lists of names, environment or configuration variables, complex data structures that represent a single underlying process, and other programming objects that are referred to as *singletons* in software engineering. In Python, because they have to be explicitly named in a declaration there is a constant reminder of the variable's scope.

Variable Parameter Lists

The **print()** function is interesting because it seems to be able to accept any number of parameters and deal with them. The statement:

```
print(i)
```

prints the value of the variable **i**, and

```
print (i,j,k)
```

prints the value of all three variables **i**, **j**, and **k**. Is this some sort of special thing reserved for **print()** because Python knows about it? Nope. Any function can do this. Consider a function:

```
fprint ( "format string", variable list)
```

where the format string can contain the characters "f" or "i" in any combination. Each instance of a letter should correspond to a variable passed to the function in the variable list, and it will be printed as a floating point if the corresponding character in the format string is "f" and as an integer if it is "i." The call:

```
fprint("fi", 12, 13)
```

will print the values 12 and 13 as a float and an integer respectively. How can this be written as a Python function?

The function would start out with the following definition:

```
def fprint (fstring, *vlist)
```

The expression ***vlist** represents a set of positional parameters, any number of them. This is preceded by a specific parameter **fstring**, which will be the format string. A simple test of this would be to just print the variables in the list to see if it works:

```
def fprint (fstring, *vlist)
    for v in vlist:
        print v
```

When called as fprint("", 12, 13, 14, 15) this prints:

```
12
13
14
15
```

It removes some of the magic to point out that what is going on is that the list of variable after the ° character is turned into a tuple which is passed as the parameter, so the °**vlist** actually counts as a single parameter with many components. No magic.

To finish the original function, what has to be done is to peel characters off of the front of the format string, match them against a variable, and print the result as the format character dictates. So use the same loop as above, but also an index into the format string increases each time through and is used to indicate the format. It is also important that the number of format items equals the number of variables:

```
def fprint (s, *vlist):
    i = 0
    if len(s) != len(vlist):    # Format string and variable
                                   list agree?
        print ("There must be the same number of
               variables as format items.")
        return
    for v in vlist:             # For each variable
        if s[i] == "f":         # Is the corresponding format
                                   'f'?
            fv = float(v)       # Yes. Make it a float
            print (fv, " ", end="")   # . . . and print it
        elif s[i] == "i":       # Is the corresponding format
                                   'i'?
            iv = int(v)         # Yes. Make it an integer
            print(iv, " ", end="")    # . . . and print it
        else:
            print ("?", end="")      # Don't know what
                                       this is. Print it
        i = i + 1
```

All of the known positional parameters must come before the variable list; otherwise, the end of the variable list can't be determined. There is a second complication, that being the existence of *named* parameters. Those are indicated by a parameter such as °°**nlist**. The two "°" characters indicate a list of named variables. This is properly a more advanced topic.

Variables as Functions

Because Python is effectively untyped and variables can represent any kind of thing at all, a variable can be made to refer to a function; not the function name itself, which always refers to a specific function, but a variable that can be made to refer to *any* function. Consider the following functions, each of which does one trivial thing:

```
def print0():
    print ("Zero")
def print1():
    print ("One")
def print2():
    print ("Two")
def print3():
    print("Three")
```

Now make a variable reference one of these functions by means of an assignment statement:

```
printNum = print1       # Note that there is no parameter list
                        given
```

The variable **printNum** now represents a function, and when invoked the function it represents will be invoked. So:

```
printNum()
```

will result in the output:

```
One
```

Why did the statement printNum = print1 not result in the function print1 being called? Because the parameter list was absent. The statement:

```
printNum = print1()
```

results in a call to print1 at that moment, and the value of the variable printNum will be the return value of the function. This is the essential syntactic difference: print1 is a function value, and print1() is a call to the function. To emphasize this point, here is some code that would allow the English name of a number between 1 and 3 to be printed:

```
if a == 1:
  printNum = print1       # Assign the function print1 to printNum
elif a == 2:
```

```
   printNum = print2     # Assign the function print2 to printNum
   else:
   printNum = print3     # Assign the function print3 to printNum

       . . .

   printNum()            # Call the function represented by
                         printNum
```

There are more subtle uses in this case. Consider this use of a list:

```
a = 1
printList = [print0, print1, print2, print3]
printNum = printList[a]
printNum()
```

will result in the output:

```
One
```

The final iteration of this is to call the function directly from the list:

```
printList[1]()
```

This works because printList[1] is a function, and a function call is a function followed by (). Seems overly complicated, doesn't it? It is rarely used.

For those with an interest or need for mathematics, consider a function that computes the derivative or integral of another function. Passing the function to be differentiated or integrated as a parameter may be the best way to proceed in these cases.

Example: Find the Maximum Value of a Function

Maximizing a function can have important consequences in real life. The function may represent how much money will be made by manufacturing various objects, how many patients can get through an emergency ward in an hour, or how much food will be grown with a particular crop. If the function is

Why? well-behaved, then there are many mathematically sound ways to find a maximum or minimum value, but if a function is harder to deal with, then less analytical methods may have to be used. This problem proposes a search for the best pair of parameters to a problem that could be solved using a method called *linear programming*.

The problem goes like this:

> A calculator company produces a scientific calculator and a
> graphing calculator. Long-term projections indicate an expected
> demand of at least 100 scientific and 80 graphing calculators
> each day. Because of limitations on production capacity, no more
> than 200 scientific and 170 graphing calculators can be made daily.
> To satisfy a shipping contract, a total of at least 200 calculators
> much be shipped each day.
>
> If each scientific calculator sold results in a $2 loss, but each
> graphing calculator produces a $5 profit, how many of each type
> should be made daily to maximize net profits?

Let **s** be the number of scientific calculators manufactured and **g** be the
number of graphing calculators. From the problem statement:

$$100 <= s <= 200$$
$$80 <= g <= 170$$

Also:

$$s + g \geq 200, \quad \text{or} \quad g \geq 200 - s$$

Finally, the profit, which is to be maximized, is:

$$P = -2s + 5g$$

First, code the profit as a function:

```
def profit (s, g):
    return -2*s + 5*g
```

A search through the range of possibilities will run through all possible
values of s and all possible values of g; that is, s from 100 to 200 and g from
80 to 170. The function will be evaluated at each point and the maximum
will be remembered:

```
# Range for s is x0 .. x1
# Range for g is y0 .. y1
# s+g must be >= sum
def searchmax (f, x0, y0, x1, y1, sum):
    pmax = -1.0e12
    ps = -100
    pg = -100
    for s in range (x0, x1+1):        # For all possible s
        for g in range (y0, y1+1):    # For all possible g
```

```
        if s+g >= sum:          # Condition is ok?
            p = f (s, g)        # Calculate the profit.
            if p>=pmax:         # Best so far?
                pmax = p        # Yes.
                ps = s          # Save it and
                pg = g          #   the parameters
    return ( (ps, pg) )
```

Finally, the call that does the optimization calls the search function passing the profit function as a parameter:

```
c = searchmax (profit, 100, 80, 200, 170, 200)
print (c)
```

The answer found is the tuple (100, 170), or s=100 and g = 170, which agrees with the correct answer as found by other methods. This is only one example of the value of being able to pass functions as parameters. Most of the code that does this is mathematical, but it may accomplish practical tasks like optimizing performance, drawing graphs and charts, and simulating real-world events.

Functions as Return Values

Just as any value, including a function, can be stored in a variable, any value, including a function, can be returned by a function. If a function that prints an English name of a number is desired, it could be returned by a function:

```
def print0():
    print ("Zero")
def print1():
    print ("One")
def print2():
    print ("Two")
def print3():
    print("Three")
def getPrintFun (a):    # Return a function to print a numeric
                          value 0..3
if a == 0:
    return print0  # Return the function print0 as the result
elif a == 1:
    return print1  # Return the function print1 as the result
elif a == 2:
    return print2  # Return the function print2 as the result
else:
    return print3  # Return the function print3 as the result
```

Calling this function and assigning it to a variable means returning a function that can print a numerical value:

```
printNum = getPrintFun(2) # Assign a function to printNum
```

and then:

```
printNum()    # Call the function represented by printNum
```

results in the output:

```
Two
```

The function **printFun** returns, as a value, the function to be called to print that particular number. Returning the name of the function returns something that can be called.

Why would any of these seemingly odd aspects of Python be useful? Allowing a general case, permitting the most liberal interpretation of the language, would permit unanticipated applications, of course. And the ability to use a function as a variable value and a return result are a natural consequence of Python having no specific type connected with a variable at compilation time. There are many specific reasons to use functions in this way, on the other hand. Imagine a function that plots a graph. Being able to pass this function another function to be plotted is surely the most general way to accomplish its task.

Recursion

Python functions can be recursive. *Recursion* refers to a way of defining things and a programming technique, not a general language feature. Something that is recursive is defined at least partly in terms of itself. When talking about functions, a function is recursive if it contains within it a call to itself. This is normally done only when the thing that it is attempting to accomplish has a definition that is recursive. Recursion as a programming technique is an attempt to make the solution simpler. If it does not, then it is inappropriate to use recursion.

Each call to a function can be thought of as an instance of that function, and it will create all of the local variables that are declared within it. Each instance has its own copy of these, including its parameters, and each call returns to the caller as occurs with any other function call.

One important use of recursion is in reducing a problem into smaller parts, each of which has a simpler solution than does the whole problem. An example of this is searching a list for an item. If **names = [Adams, Alira, Attenbourough, . . .]** is a Python list of names in alphabetical order, answer the question: "Does the name *Parker* appear in this list?" Of course these is a built-in function that will do this, but this example is a pedagogical moment, and anyway perhaps the built-in function is slower than the solution that will be devised here.

The function will return **True** or **False** when passed a list and a name. The obvious way to solve the problem is to iterate through the list, looking at all of the elements until the name being searched for is either found or it is not possible to find it anymore (i.e., the current name in the list is larger than the target name). Another, less obvious way to conduct the search is to divide the list in half, and only search the half that has the target name in it. Consider the following names in the list:

. . . Broadbent   Butterworth Cait Cara Carling Devers Dillan Eberly Foxworthy . . .

The name in the middle if this list is *Carling*. If the name being searched for is lexicographically smaller than *Carling*, then it must appear in the first half; otherwise, it must appear in the second half. That is, if it is there at all. A recursive example of an implementation of this is:

```
# Search the list for the given name, recursively.
def searchr (name, nameList):
    n = len(nameList)          # How many elements in this list?
    m = n/2
    if name < nameList[m]:     # target name is in the first half
        return searchr (name, nameList[0:m])
# Search the first half
    elif name > nameList[m]:   # target must be in the second
                               half
        return searchr (name, nameList[m:n])
                               # Search the second half
    else:
        return True
```

If the name is in the list, this works fine. One way to think of this is that the function **searchr()** will take a string and a list as parameters and find the name in the list if it's there. The way it works is not clear from outside the function (without being able to see the source) and should not matter. So, if the target is to be found in the first half of the list, for example, then call **searchr()** with the first half of the list.

```
searchr (name, nameList[0:m])
```

The fact that the call is recursive is not really the concern of the programmer, but it is the concern of the person who created the Python system. Now, how can the problem of a name not being in the list be solved?

When the name is not in the list, the program will continue until there is but one item in the list. If that item is not the target, then it is not to be found. So, if n=1 (only one item in the list) and **nameList[0]** is not equal to the target, then the target is not to be found in the list and the return value should be **False**. The final program will therefore be:

```
def searchr (name, nameList):
    n = len(nameList)        # How many elements in this list?
    m = int(n/2)

    if n==1 and nameList[0]!=name:    # End of the recursive
                                      calls
        return False                  # It's not in this list.
    if name < nameList[m]:   # target name is in the first half
        return searchr (name, nameList[0:m])
                             # Search the first half
    elif name > nameList[m]:
                             # target must be in the second half
        return searchr (name, nameList[m:n])
                             # Search the second half
    else:
        return True
```

Many algorithms have fundamentally recursive implementations, meaning that the effective solution in code involves a recursive function call. Examples of very useful recursive functions will be examined in later chapters.

Creating a Python Module

In some of the examples given so far there is a statement at the beginning that looks like "import name." The implication is that there are some functions that are needed by the program that are provided elsewhere, possibly by the Python system itself or perhaps by some other software developer. The idea of writing functions that can be reused in a straightforward way is very important to the software development process. It means that no programmer is really alone, that code is available for doing things like generating random numbers or interfacing with the operating system or the Internet, and that it does not need to be created each time. In addition, there is an assumption that a module *works correctly*. When a programmer builds a collection of code for their own use, it needs to be tested as thoroughly as possible, and from that time on it can be used in a package with confidence. If a program has errors in it, then look in the code for that program first and not in the modules. This makes debugging code faster.

What is a module? It is simply a function or collection of functions that reside in a file whose name ends in ".py." Technically, all of the code developed so far qualifies as modules. Consider as an example the function from the previous section that finds the maximum value in a list. Save the functions **max()** and **maxr()** in a file named ***max.py***. Now create a new Python program named ***usemax.py*** and place it in the same directory as ***max.py***. If the two files are in the same directory, then they can "see" each other in some sense.

Here is some code to place in the file ***usemax.py***:

```
import max
d = [12,32,76,45,9,26,84,25,61, 66, 1,2]
print ("MAX is ", max.max(d), " MAXR is ", max.maxr(d))
if max.maxr(d) != max.max(d):
    print ("*** NOT EQUAL ****")
```

This program is just a test of the two functions to make certain that they return the same value for the same list, the variable **d**. Note two things:

1) The statement **import max** occurs at the beginning of the program, meaning that the code inside this file is available to this program. Python will look inside of this file for function and variable names.
2) When the function **max()** or **maxr()** is called, the function name is preceded by the module name (**max**) and a period. This syntax informs the Python system that the name **maxr()** (for example) is found in the module **max** and not elsewhere.

The first time that the module is loaded into the Python program, the code in the module is executed. This allows any variable initializations to be performed. Henceforth that code is not executed again, and functions within the module can be called knowing that the initializations have been performed.

The module could reside in the same directory as the program that uses it, but it does not have to. The Python system recognizes a set of directories and paths, and modules can be placed in some of those locations as well, making it easier for other programs on the same computer to take advantage of them. On the computer used to create the examples in this book, the directory C:\Python34\Lib can be used to store modules, and they will be recognized by **import** statements.

Finally, if the syntax **max.maxr(list)** seems a bit cumbersome, then it is possible to import specific names from the module into the program. Consider the following rewrite of **usemax.py**:

```
from max import max, maxr
d = [12,32,76,45,9,26,84,25,61, 66, 1,2]
print ("MAX is ", max(d), " MAXR is ", maxr(d))
if maxr(d) != max(d):
    print ("*** NOT EQUAL ****")
```

The statement **from max import max, maxr** instructs Python to recognize the names **max** and **maxr** as belonging to the module named max (i.e., as residing in the file named **max.py**). In that case the function can be called by simply referencing their names.

## CHAPTER 5

FILES: INPUT AND OUTPUT

The first thing to know about a file is that it is a collection of bytes stored on a disk or similar device. One set of bytes can look very much like another, and unless the format of the file (i.e., the way the bytes are ordered) and its basic contents (i.e., what kind of thing the bytes represent) is known ahead of time, the information stored there is unusable. Computer programs are written assuming that the files they will read have a particular nature; if given a file that does not have that nature, the program will not function properly.

What kinds of files are there? Here is a short list:

- Text files. These contain characters that a person can read, and can be thought of as documents.
- Executable files. These hold instructions that a computer can execute. Such a file is a program or an "app."
- Data files. It could also be a text file if it is stored as characters, but it could be a set of bytes that represents integers or real numbers.
- Image files. There are many types of image files, and they contain pictures in digital format. Many digital cameras use a format called JPEG, but GIF or PNG are two of many others. Not only are images stored in such a file, but also data about how large the image is, when it was taken, and other details.
- Sound files. The more common sound file is the MP3, but there are many others.

- Video. MPEG and AVI are standard formats for video, and there are a great many files of this sort available on the Internet.
- Web pages. These are a special kind of text file. They can be examined and modified using basic text editors, but can't be viewed properly (i.e., as a web page) except through a browser, which is really a special kind of display utility that can both draw images and connect to the Internet to download more information.

All of these files, and indeed all files, have certain things in common. Some of these things can be ignored when writing Python programs, but others cannot.

Files have names. The first way to access a file is usually by specifying its name.

Files have a size. It is usually expressed in bytes, which is to say characters.

Basic operations on a file are *read* and *write*. To read from a file means to examine a byte (at least). Writing is the reverse process: a byte or bytes are copied from memory onto disk.

Files must be *open* before they can be used. To open a file a program must know its name, and then invoke the *open* function or program. The *open* function and many other file-related operations belong to the operating system of the computer, and not normally to the language. It's one reason why so much software is not portable.

Only one program at a time can write to a file. Many programs can read a file simultaneously, but only one can write to it, and not while anyone else is reading it.

Another thing to consider is that text, and therefore text files, are a principal means for communication between humans and computers. It is critical that any scheme for writing text to a file takes into account the human aspects of text: sentences, lines, paragraphs, special characters, numbers, and so on. This chapter will be concerned with the way in which Python can use files, with files as a concept in general, and with how humans think of data and files.

How long does it take to access a block of data on the disk? The time to access a random data item can be estimated as 14.15 *milliseconds*. Disk is vastly slower than memory, and in order to use the data, it must be copied into memory. This is a bottleneck in many computer systems.

Problem: Read a Number from the Keyboard and Divide It by 2

In this instance the problem is one of type: how to treat integers like integers and floats like floats. When the string **s** is read in it's just a string, and it is supposed to contain an integer. However, users will be users, and some may type in a float by mistake. The program should not crash just because of a simple inputting mistake. How is this situation handled?

The problem is that when the string is converted into an integer, if there is a decimal point or other non-digit character that does not belong then an error will occur. It seems that an answer would be to put the conversion into a **try** statement block and if the string has a decimal point then convert the string to float within the **except** part. Something like this:

```
s = input("Input an integer: ")
try:
    k = int(s)
    ks = k//2
except:
    z = float(s)
    k = int(z/2)
print (k)
```

If the user types "12" in response to the prompt "Input an integer: " then the program prints "6." If the user types "12.5" then the program catches a **ValueError**, because 12.5 is not a legal integer. The except part is executed, converting the number to floating point, dividing by 2, then finally converting to an integer.

One problem is that the **except** part is not part of the **try**, so errors that happen there will not be caught. Imagine that the user types "one" in response to the prompt. The call to **int(s)** results in a **ValueError**, and the **except** part is executed. The statement:

```
z = float(s)
```

will result in another **ValueError**. This one will not be caught and the program will stop executing, giving a message like:

```
ValueError: could not convert string to float: 'one'
s = input("Input an integer: ")
try:
    k = int(s)
    k = k//2
```

```
    except ValueError:
        try:
            z = float(s)
            k = int(z/2)
        except ValueError:
            k = 0
print (s, k)
```

Using Files in Python

The general paradigm for reading and writing files is the same in Python as it is in most other languages. The steps for reading or writing a file are these:

1) **Open the file**. This involves calling a function, usually named **open**, and passing the name of the file to be used. Sometimes the *mode* for opening is passed; that is, a file can be opened for input, output, update (both input and output), and in binary modes. The function locates the file using the name and returns a variable that keeps track of the current state of input from the file. A special case exists if there is no file having the given name.

2) **Read data from the file**. Using the variable returned by **open**, a function is called to read data. The function might read a character, or a number, or a line, or the whole file. The function is often called **read**, and can be called multiple times. The next call to **read** will read from where the last call ended. A special case exists when all of the data has been read from the file (Called the *end of file* condition).

   OR

2) **Write data to the file**. Using the variable returned by **open**, a function is called to write data to the file. The function might write a character, or a number, or a line, or many lines. The function is often called **write**, and can be called multiple times. The next call to **write** will continue writing data from where the last call ended. Writing data most frequently appends data to the end of the file.

3) **Close the file**. Closing a file is also accomplished using a call to a function (yes, it is usually named **close**). This function frees storage associated with the input process and in some cases unlocks the file so it can be used by other programs. A variable returned by **open** is passed to **close**, and afterwards that variable can't be used for input anymore. The file is no longer open.

Open a File

Python provides a function named **open** that will open a file and return a value that can be used to read from or write to the file. That value actually refers to a complex collection of values that refers to the file status and is called a *handle* or a *file descriptor* in the computing literature, although knowledge of the details is not needed to use it. It can be thought of as something of type *file*, and must be assigned to a variable or the file can't be accessed. The **open** function is given the name of the file to be opened and a flag that indicates whether the file is to be read from or written to. Both of these are strings. A simple example of a call to open is:

```
infile = open ("datafile.txt", "r")
```

This will open a file named "datafile.txt" that resides in the same directory as does the Python program, and opens it for input: the "r" flag means *read*. It returns the handle to the variable **infile**, which can now be used to read data from the file.

There are some details that are crucial. The name of the file on most computer systems can be a path name, which is to say the name including all directory names that are used to find it on your computer. For example, on some computers the name "datafile.txt" might have the complete path name "C:/parker/introProgramming/chapter05/datafile.txt." If path names are used, the file can be opened from any directory on the computer. This is handy for large data sets that are used by multiple programs, such as names of customers or suppliers.

The *read* flag "r" that is the second parameter is what was called the mode in the previous discussion. The "r" flag means that the file will be open for reading only, and starts reading at the beginning of the file. The default is to read characters from the file, which is presumed to be a text file. Opening with the mode "rb" opens the file in binary format, and allows reading non-text files, such as MP3 and video files.

Passing the mode "w" means that the file is to be written to. If the file exists, then it will be overwritten; if not, the file will be created. Using "wb" means that a binary file is to be written.

Append mode is indicated by the mode parameter "a," and it means that the file will be opened for writing, and if the file exists then writing will begin at the end of the existing file. In other words, the file will not start over as being empty but will be added to, at the end of the file. The mode "ab" appends data to a binary file. There are a few other modes that will be discussed when they are needed.

If the file does not exist and it is being opened for input, there is a problem. It's an error, of course; a nonexistent file can't be read from. There are ways to tell whether a file exists, and the error caused by a non-existent file can be caught and handled from within Python. This involves an **exception**. It is always a bad idea to assume that everything works properly, and when dealing with files it is especially important to check for all likely problems.

File Not Found Exceptions

The proper way to open a file is within a **try-except** pair of statements. This will ensure that nonexistent files or permission errors are caught rather than causing the program to terminate. The basic scheme is simple:

```
try:
        infile = open ("datafile.txt", "r")
except FileNotFoundError:
    print ("There is no file named 'datafile.txt'. Please try again")
        return      # end program or abort this section of code
```

The exception **FileNotFoundError** will be thrown if the file name can't be found. What to do in that case depends on the program: if the file name was typed in by the user, then perhaps they should get another chance. In any case the file is not open, and data can't be read.

There are multiple versions of Python on computers around the world, and some versions have different names for things. The examples here all use Python 3.4. In other versions the **FileNotFoundError** exception has another name; it may be **IOError** or even **OSError**. The documentation for the version being used should be consulted if a compilation error occurs when using exceptions and some built-in functions. For the 3.4 compiler version, all three seem to work with a missing file.

All attempts to open a file should take place while catching the **FileNotFoundError** exception.

Reading from Files

After a file is opened with a read mode, the file descriptor returned can be used to read data from the file. Using the variable **infile** returned from the call to **open** () above, a call to the method **read**() can get a character from the file:

```
s = infile.read(1)
```

Reading one character at a time is always good enough, but is inefficient. If a block on disk is 512 characters (bytes), then that should be a good number of bytes to read at one time, or a multiple of that. Reading more data than you need and saving it is called *buffering*, and buffers are used in many instances: live video and audio streaming, audio players, and even in programming language compilers. The idea is to read a larger block of data than is needed at the moment and to hand it out as needed. Reading a buffer could be done as:

```
s = infile.read(512)
```

and then dealing characters from the strings one at a time as needed. A buffer is a collection of memory locations that is temporary storage for data that was recently on secondary store.

Text files, those that contain printable characters that humans can read, are normally arranged as lines separated by a carriage return or a linefeed character, something usually called a *newline*. An entire line can be read using the **readline**() function:

```
s = infile.readline()
```

A line is not usually a sentence, so many lines might be needed to read one sentence, or perhaps only half of a line. Computer text files are structured so that humans can read them, but the structure of human language and convention is not understood by the computer nor it is built into the file structure. However, it is normal for people to make data files that contain data for a particular item or event on one line, followed by data for the next item. If this is true then one call to **readline**() will return all of the information for a particular thing.

End of File

When there are no more characters in the file, **read**() will return the empty string: "". This is called the *end of file condition*, and it is important that it be detected. There are many ways to open and read files, but for reading characters in this way the end of file is checked as follows:

```
infile = open("data.txt", "r")
while True:
  c = infile.read(1)
```

```
    if c == '':
        print ("End of file")
        exit()
    else:
        c = infile.read(1)
```

When reading a file in a **for** statement, the end of file is handled automatically. In this case the loop runs from the first line to the final line and then stops.

```
for c in f:
    print ("'", c, "'")
```

Oddly an exception can't be used in an obvious way for handling the end of file on file input. However, when reading from the console using the input() function, the exception **EOFError** can be caught:

```
while True:
    try:
        c = input()
        print (c)
    except EOFError:
        print ("Endfile")
        break
```

There are many errors that could occur for any set of statements. It is possible to determine what specific exception has been thrown in the following manner:

```
while True:
    try:
        c = input()
        print (c)
    except Exception as x:
        print (x)
        break
```

This code prints "EOF when reading a line" when the end of file is encountered.

Common File Input Operations

There are a few common ways to use files that should be mentioned as *patterns*. Although one should never use a pattern if it is not understood, it's sometimes handy to have a few simple snippets of code that are known to perform basic tasks correctly. For example, one common operation to use with files is to **read each line from a file**, followed by some processing step. This looks like:

```
f = open ("data.txt", "r")
for c in f:
    print ("'", c, "'")
f.close()
```

The expression **c in f** results in consecutive lines being read from the files into a string variable **c**, and this stops when no more data can be read from the file.

Another way to do the same thing would be to use the **readline**() function:

```
f = open ("data.txt", "r")
c = f.readline()
while c != '':
    print ("'", c, "'")
    c = f.readline()
f.close()
```

In this case the end of file has to be determined explicitly, by checking the string value that was read to see if it is null.

CSV Files

A very common format for storing data is called Comma Separated Variable (CSV) format, named for the fact that each pair of data items have a comma between them. CSV files can be used directly by spreadsheets such as Excel and by a large collection of data analysis tools, so it is important to be able to read them correctly.

A simple CSV file named *planets.txt* is provided for experimenting with reading CSV files. It contains some basic data for the planets in Earth's solar system, and while there is no actual standard for how CSV files must look, this one is typical of what is usually seen. The first line in the file contains headings for each of the variables or columns, separated by commas. This is followed by nine lines of data, one for each planet.

It's a small data file as these things are counted, but illustrative for the purpose. Here it is:

Name,	Mass,	Diam,	Density,	Grav,	Escape,	Rotation,	Day,	Distance,	Period,	Moons,	Temp
Mercury,	0.364,	3032,	339,	12.1,	2.7,	1407.6,	4222.6,	36.0,	88.0,	0,	333
Venus,	5.37,	7521,	327,	29.1,	6.4,	-5832.5,	2802.0,	67.2,	224.7,	0,	867
Earth,	6.58,	7926,	344,	32.1,	7.0,	23.9,	24.0,	93.0,	365.2,	1,	59
Mars,	0.708,	4221,	246,	12.1,	3.1,	24.6,	24.7,	141.6,	687.0,	2,	-85
Jupiter,	2093,	88846,	83,	75.9,	37.0,	9.9,	9.9,	483.8,	4331.0,	67,	-166
Saturn,	627,	31783,	43,	29.4,	22.1,	10.7,	10.7,	890.8,	10747,	62,	-220
Uranus,	95.7,	31763,	79,	28.5,	13.2,	-17.2,	17.2,	1784.8,	30589,	27,	-320
Neptune,	113.0,	30775,	102,	36.0,	14.6,	16.1,	16.1,	2793.1,	59800,	14,	-330
Pluto,	0.0161,	1464,	131,	2.3,	0.8,	-153.3,	153.3,	3670.0,	90560,	5,	-375

Problem: Print the Names of Planets Having Fewer than Ten Moons

This is not a very profound problem, and uses the raw data as it appears on the file. The file must be opened and then each line of data is read; the value of the 11th data element (i.e., index 10) is retrieved and compared against 10. If larger, the name of the planet (index 0) is printed. The plan is:

Open the file
Read (skip over) the header line
For each planet
Read a line as string **s**
Break **s** into components based on commas giving list **P**
If **P[10]** < **10** print the planet name, which is **P[0]**

It is all something that has been done before except for breaking the string into parts based on the comma. Fortunately the designers of Python anticipated this kind of problem and have provided a very useful function: **split()**. This function breaks up a string into parts using a specified delimiter character or string and returns a list in which each component is one section of the fractured string. For example:

```
s = "This is a string"
z = s.split(" ")
```

yields the list z = ["This", "is", "a", "string"]. It splits the string **s** into substrings at each space character. A call like **s.split(",")** should give substrings that are separated by a comma. Given the above sketch and the split() function, the code now pretty much writes itself.

```
try:
# Open the file
    infile = open ("planets.txt", "r")
# Read (skip over) the header line
    s =infile.readline()
# For each planet
    for i in range (0, 8):
# Read a line as string s
        s = infile.readline()
# Break s into components based on commas giving list P
        P = s.split (",")
# If P[10] < 10 print the planet name, which is P[0]
        if int(P[10])<10:
            print (P[0], " has fewer than 10 moons.")
except FileNotFoundError:
        print ("There is no file named 'planets.txt'.
Please try again")
```

Things to notice: almost the entire program resides within a try statement, so that if the file does not exist, then a message will be printed and the program will end normally. Also note that P[10] has to be converted into an integer, because all components of the list P are strings. Strings are what has been read from the file.

CSV files are common enough so that Python provides a module for manipulating them. The module contains quite a large collection of material, and for the purposes of the *planets.py* program only the basics are needed. To avoid the details of a general package, a simpler version is included with this book: *simpleCSV* has the essentials needed to read most CSV files while being written in such a way that a beginning programmer should be able to read and understand it.

To use it, the **simpleCSV** module is first imported. This makes two important functions available: **nextRecord()** and **getData()**. The **nextRecord()** function reads one entire line of CSV data. It allows skipping lines without examining them in detail (like headers). The function **getData()** will parse one line of data, the last one read, into a tuple, each element of which is one of the comma separated fields.

The *simpleCSV* library needs to be in the same directory as the program that uses it, or be in the standard Python directory for installed modules. The source code resides on the accompanying disk and is called *simpleCSV.py*. The program above can be rewritten to use the *simpleCSV* module as follows:

```
import simpleCSV
try:                        # Read (skip over) the header line
```

```
    # Open the file
        infile = open ("planets.txt", "r")
      simpleCSV.nextRecord(infile)              # Read the header
      for i in range (0, 8):                    # For each planet
          simpleCSV.nextRecord(infile)  # Read a line and collect
                                                    substrings in a list
         p = simpleCSV.getData(infile)
         if int(P[10])<10:                # If number of moons less than 10
             print (P[0], " has fewer than 10 moons.") # print
                                                       the planet name
      except FileNotFoundError:
           print ("There is no file named 'planets.txt'.
                                             Please try again")
```

The With Statement

A difficulty with the code presented so far is that it does not clean up after itself. A file should be closed after input from it or output to it is finished; none of the programs written so far do that, at least not after the file operations are complete. There has been no significant discussion of the **close**() operation, but what it does has been described. Normally when a program terminates, its resources are returned to the system, including the closing of any open files. Intentionally closing a file is important for three reasons: first, if the program aborts for some reason, open files *should* be closed by the system but may not be, and file problems can be the result. Second, closing a file can be used as a step in reusing it. Opening it again starts reading it at the beginning. Third, closing a file frees its resources. Programs that use many files and/or many resources will profit from freeing them when they are no longer needed.

The Python *with* statement, in its simplest form, takes care of many of the details surrounding file access. An example of its use is:

```
try:
    with open ("planets.txt") as infile:    # Open the file
        simpleCSV.nextRecord(infile)    # Read the header
        for i in range (0, 9):         # For each planet
            simpleCSV.nextRecord(infile)  # Read a line, make a
                                                          list
            P = simpleCSV.getData(infile)
            if int(P[10])<10:                # If number of moons
                                                   less than 10
                print (P[0], " has fewer than 10 moons.")
                                               # print the name
```

```
except FileNotFoundError:
        print ("There is no file named 'planets.txt'.
                                Please try again")
```

Once the file is open, the *with* statement guarantees that certain errors will be dealt with and the file will be closed. The problem is that the file has to be open first, so the **FileNotFound** error should still be caught as an exception.

Writing to Files

The first step in writing to a file is opening it, but this time for output:

```
outfile = open ("out.txt", "w")
```

The "w" as the second parameter to **open()** means to open the file for writing. When writing to a file it is important to note that opening it will create a new file by default. If a file with the given name already exists, it will be rewritten, and the previous contents will be gone.

The basic file output function is **write()**; it takes a parameter, a string to be written to the file. It only writes strings, so numbers and other types have to be converted into strings before being written. Also, there is no concept of a line. This function simply moves characters to a file, one at a time, in the order given. In order to write a line, an end of line character has to be written. This is usually specified in a string as "\n," spoken as "backslash n." The "n" stands for newline.

Example: Write a Table of Squares to a File

This will illustrate the typical code involved in writing to a file. The file must be opened, then a loop from 0 to 25 is constructed. Each number in that range is written to the file, as is that number multiplied by itself. Each output string represents a line, and so must have a newline character added to the end.

```
outfile = open ("out.txt", "w")
outfile.write ("    X                X squared \n")
for i in range (0, 25):
    sout = "    "+str(i)+"                "+str(i*i)+"\n"
```

```
    outfile.write (sout)
outfile.close()
```

Note that the integers are explicitly converted into strings and concate-
nated into a line to be written. The elements of the line could be written
in separate calls to write:

```
outfile = open ("out.txt", "w")
outfile.write ("    X              X squared \n")
for i in range (0, 25):
    outfile.write ("    ")
    outfile.write (str(i))
    outfile.write ("            ")
    outfile.write (str(i*i))
    outfile.write ("\n")
outfile.close()
```

The output file is closed after all data has been written.

Another common file operation is to **copy a file to another**, character
by character. A file is opened for input and another for output. The basic
"read a file" pattern is used, with the addition of a file output after each
character is read:

```
f = open ("data.txt", "r")
g = open ("copy.txt", "w")
c = f.read(1)
while c != '':
    g.write(c)
    c = f.readline(1)
f.close()
g.close()
```

Two files can be merged into a single file in many ways: one file after
another, a line from one file followed by a line from another, character by
character, and so on. A simple merging of two files where one is copied
first followed by the other is:

```
f = open ("data1.txt", "r")
outfile = open ("copy.txt", "w")
c = f.read()
outfile.write(c)
f.close()
g = open ("data2.txt", "r")
```

```
c = g.read()
outfile.write(c)
g.close()
outfile.close()
```

Copying the input from console to a file means reading each line using **input**() and writing it to the file. This code assumes that an empty input line implies that the copying is complete.

```
outfile = open ("copy.txt", "w")
line = input ("! ")
while len(line)>1 or line[0]!="!":
    outfile.write(line)
    outfile.write ("\n")
    line = input("! ")
outfile.close()
```

The end of the line is indicated by a character, which is represented by the string "\n." Reading characters from a file will read the end of line character also, and detecting it can be very important.

```
f = open ("data.txt", "r")
c = f.read(1)
while c != '':
    print ("'", c, "'")
    c = f.read(1)
    if c == '\n':
        print ("Newline")
```

Appending Data to a File

Opening the file in "w" mode starts writing at the beginning of the file, and will result in existing data being lost. This is not always desirable. For example, what if a log file is being created? The log should contain a record of everything that has happened, not just the most recent thing.

Opening the file in *append* mode, signified by the parameter "a," opens the file for output and starts writing at the end of the file if it already exists. This means that data can be added to the end of an existing file.

Example: Append Another 20 Squares to the Table of Squares File

The previous example created a file named "out.txt" and wrote 26 lines to it. It was a table of squares, and the final one was 24. This example will therefore begin at 25 and add 20 more values to the table.

The main difference is the opening of the output file in append mode, and starting the loop at 25 instead of at 0:

```
outfile = open ("out.txt", "a")
for i in range (25, 45):
    sout = "     "+str(i)+"          "+str(i*i)+"\n"
    outfile.write (sout)
outfile.close()
```

The file "out.txt" will contain the squares of the integers between 0 and 44 inclusive after this program runs.

6

CLASSES

A **class**, in the general sense, *is a template for something that involves data and operations (functions)*. An **object** is *an instance of a class, a specific instantiation of the template*. Defining a class in Python involves specifying a class name and a collection of variables and functions that will belong to that class. The main class that has been referred to so far has only a few characteristics that we know about for certain.

Consider the joke that begins with the phrase "A man walks into a bar"? What is a *man*, what is a *bar*, and what does *walking* entail? *Walking* seems to be something that a man can do, an action they can perform. And a *bar* is a place where a *man* can *walk*. Can a *man* do anything else but *walk*? Is a *bar* the only place a man can *walk* to?

A *man* could be a class. It does have a function called **walksInto**, as one example. A first draft of the man class could be as follows:

```
class man:
    def walksInto (aBar):
        # code goes here
```

In the above example **walksInto** is a method; essentially, a method is any function that is part of a class.

Classes can have their own data too, which would be variables that "belong" to the class in that they exist inside it. Such variables can be used inside the class but can't be seen from outside.

Looking closely at the simple class **man** above, notice that it is actually still a rather abstract thing. In the narrative about a man walking into a bar it was a specific *man*, as indicated by a variable **aMan**. So it would seem that a class is really a description of something, and that examples or instances should be created in order to make use of that description. This is correct. In fact, many individual instances of any class can be created (instantiated) and assigned to variables. To create a new instance of the class **man**, the following syntax could be used:

```
aMan = man()
```

When this is done all of the variables used in the definition of man are allocated. In fact, whenever a new man class is created, a special method that is local to man is called to initialize variables. This method is the *constructor*, and can take parameters that help in the initialization. Creating a man might involve giving him a name, so the instantiation may be:

```
aMan = man("Jim Parker")
```

In this case the constructor accepts a parameter, a string, and probably assigns it to a variable local to the class (**Name**, most likely). The constructor is always named **__init__**:

```
def __init__ (self, parameter1, parameter2, . . .):
```

The initial parameter named **self** is a reference to the class being defined. Any variable that is a part of this class is referred to by prefixing the variable name with "self." To make a constructor for **man** that accepted a name, it would look like this:

```
def __init__ (self, name):
    self.Name = name
```

When a man is created, the statement would be:

```
        aMan = man ("Jim Parker")
```

This metaphor has fulfilled its purpose for the moment.

The Python Class – Syntax and Semantics

The *man walks into a bar* example illustrates many aspects of the Python class structure but obviously omits many details, especially formal ones that can be so important to a programmer. A **class** looks like a function in that there is a keyword, **class**, and a name and a colon, followed by an indented region of code. Everything in that indented region "belongs" to the class, and cannot be used from outside without using the class name or the name of a variable that is an instance of the class.

The method **__init__** is used to initialize any variables that belong to the class. Java would call this method a *constructor*, and that's how it will be referenced here too. Any variables that belong to the class must be accessed through either an instance (from outside of the class) or by using the name **self** (from within the class). So, **self.name** would refer to a variable that was defined inside of the class whereas simply using **name** would refer to a variable local to a method. When **__init__** is called a set of parameters can be passed and used to initialize variables in the class. If the first parameter is **self**, it means that the method can access class-local variables, otherwise it cannot. Normally self is passed to **__init__** or it can't initialize things. Any variable initialized within **__init__** and prefixed by **self** is a class-local variable. Any method that is passed **self** as a parameter can define a new class-local variable, but it makes sense to initialize all of them in one place if that's possible.

A simple example of a class, initialization, and method is:

```
class person:
    def __init__ (self, name):
        self.name = name

    def introduce (self):
        print ("Hi, my name is ", self.name)

me = person("Jim")
me.introduce()
```

This class has two methods, **__init__**() and **introduce**(). After the class is defined, a variable named **me** is defined and is given a new instance of the **person** class having the name "Jim." Then this variable is used to access the introduce method, which prints the introduction message "Hi, my name is Jim." A second instance could be created and assigned to a second variable named **you** using:

```
you = person ("Mike")
```

and the method call

```
you.introduce()
```

would result in the message "Hi, my name is Mike." Any number of instances can be created, and some may have the same name as others— they are still distinct instances.

A new class-local variable can be created by any method. In **introduce**(), for example, a new local named **introductions** can be created simply by assigning a value to it.

```
def introduce (self):
    print ("Hi, my name is ", self.name)
    self.introductions = True
```

This variable is **True** if the method introductions has been called. The main program can access this variable directly. If the main program becomes:

```
me = person("Jim")
me.introduce()
print (me.introductions)
```

then the program will generate the output:

```
Hi, my name is  Jim
True
```

This is the essential information needed to define and use a class in Python. A more complex example would be useful in seeing how these features can be used in practice.

A Really Simple Class

A common example of a basic class is a point, a place on a plane specified by x and y coordinates. The beginning of this class is:

```
class point:
    def __init__ (self, x, y):
        self.x = x
        self.y = y
```

This simply represents the data associated with a mathematical point. What more does it need? Well, two points have a distance between them. A distance method could be added to the point:

```
def distance (self, p):
    d = (self.x-p.x)*(self.x-p.x)+(self.y-p.y)*(self.y-p.y)
    return sqrt(d)
```

If a traditional function were to be used to compute distance, it would be written similarly but not identically. It would take two points as parameters:

```
def distance (p1, p2):
    d = (p1.x-p2.x)*(p1.x-p2.x) + (p1.y-p2.y)* (p1.y-p2.y)
    return sqrt(d)
```

The **distance** method uses one of the points as a preferred parameter, in a sense. The distance between points p1 and p2 would be calculated as:

```
d = p1.distance(p2) or d = p2.distance(p1)
```

using the distance method, but as:

```
d = distance (p1, p2)
```

if the function was used. To a degree the difference is a philosophical one. Is *distance* some property that a point has from another point (the method), or is it something that is a thing that is calculated for two things (the function)? A programmer begins, after a while, to see the methods and data of a class as belonging to the object, and as being somehow properties of it. That's what makes a class a type definition.

Many object-oriented languages offer the concept of *accessor* methods. All that an *accessor* method does is return a value of importance to a user of a class. The x and y positions are variables local to the class, and many would agree that they should have an *accessor* method:

```
def getx (self):
    return self.x

def gety (self):
    return self.y
```

Rewriting the **distance()** method to use accessor methods changes it only slightly:

```
def distance (self, p):
    d = (self.x-p.getx())*(self.x-p.getx()) +
        (self.y-p.gety())* (self.y-p.gety())
    return sqrt(d)
```

Methods called *mutators* or *setters* are used to modify the value of a variable in a class. They may do more than that, such as checking ranges and types, and tracking modifications.

```
def setx (self, x):
    self.x = x
def sety (self, y):
    self.y = y
```

There are other methods that could be added to even this simple class just in case they were needed, such as to draw the point, to return a string that describes the object, to rotate about the origin or some other point, a *destructor* (what to do when the object is no longer needed), and so on. Until it is known what the class will be used for there may not be any value for this effort, but if a class is being provided for general utility, like the Python *string*, as much functionality would be provided as the programmer's imagination could invent. A draw method could simply print the coordinates, and could be useful for debugging:

```
def draw (self):
    print ("(", self.x, ",", self.y, ") ")
```

Using this class involves creating instances and using the provided methods, and that should be all. A triangle consists of three points. A triangle *class* could be defined as:

```
class triangle:
    def __init__ (self, p0, p1, p2):
        self.v0 = p0
        self.v1 = p1
        self.v2 = p2
        self.x = (p0.getx()+p1.getx()+p2.getx())/3
        self.y = (p0.gety()+p1.gety()+p2.gety())/3

    def set_vertices (self, p0, p1, p2):
        self.v0 = p0
        self.v1 = p1
        self.v2 = p2

    def get_vertices (self):
      return ( (self.v0, self.v1, self.v2) )

    def getx (self):
        return self.x

    def gety (self):
        return self.y
```

The (x, y) value of a triangle is its center, or the average value of the x and the y coordinates of the vertices. These are the basic methods. A triangle is likely to be drawn somehow, and the next chapter will explain how to do that specifically. However, without knowing the details, a triangle is a set of lines drawn between the vertices and so might be done that way. As it is, using text only, it will print its vertices:

```
def draw (self):
    print ("Triangle:")
```

```
    self.v0.draw()
    self.v1.draw()
    self.v2.draw()
```

The triangle can be moved to a new position. A change in the x and y locations specifies the change, and it is done by changing the coordinates of each of the vertices:

```
def move (self, dx, dy)
    coord = p0.getx()
    p0.setx(coord+dx)
    coord = p0.gety()
    p0.sety(coord+dy)
    coord = p1.getx()
    p1.setx(coord+dx)
    coord = p0.gety()
    p1.sety(coord+dy)
    coord = p2.getx()
    p2.setx(coord+dx)
    coord = p2.gety()
    p2.sety(coord+dy)
    self.x = self.x + dx
    self.y = self.y + dy
```

In this way of expressing things, it is clear that moving the triangle is a matter of changing the coordinates of the vertices. If each point had a **move()** method, then it would be clearer: moving a triangle is a matter of moving each of the vertices:

```
def move (self, dx, dy):
    p0.move(dx, dy)
    p1.move(dx, dy)
    p2.move(dx, dy)
    self.x = self.x + dx
    self.y = self.y + dy
```

Which of these two **move()** methods seems the best description of what is happening? The more complex are the classes, the more value there is in making an effort to design them to effectively communicate their behaviors and to make things easier to expand and modify. It is also plain that the **move()** method for a point is simpler than that for a triangle. That fact is invisible from outside the class, and it is actually not relevant.

Encapsulation

In the example of the *point* class, there is no actual need for an accessor method because the variables can be accessed from outside the class, in spite of the arguments that have been given for more controlled use of these variables. A careful programmer would want to ensure the integrity of classes by forcing the variables to remain protected in some way, and Python allows this while not requiring it.

The variables x and y are accessible and modifiable from outside because of how they are named. Any variable name in a class that begins with an underscore character ('_') cannot be modified by code that does not belong to the class. Such a variable is said to be *protected*. A variable name that begins with two underscore characters can't be modified or even examined from outside of the class, and is said to be *private*. All other variables are *public*. This applies to method names too, so the method __init__() that is the usual constructor is private.

Rewriting the point class to make the internal variables private would be done like this:

```
class point:
    def __init__ (self, x, y):
        self.__x = x
        self.__y = y

def getx (self):
    return self.__x

def gety (self):
    return self.__y

det setx (self, x):
    self.__x = x

def sety (self, y):
    self.__yy = y

def distance (self, p):
    d = (self.__x-p.getx())*(self.__x-p.getx()) +
        (self.__y-p.gety())* (self.__y-p.gety())
    return sqrt(d)

def move(self, dx, dy):
    self.__x = self.__x + dx
    self.__y = self.__y + dy

def draw (self):
    print ("(", self.__x, ",", self.__y, ") ")
```

Now the internal variables x and y can't be modified or even have their values examined unless explicitly allowed by a method.

Example: A Deck of Cards

Traditional playing cards these days have red and black colors, four suits, and a total of 52 cards, 13 in each suit. Individual cards are components of a deck, and can be sorted: a 2 is less than a 3, a Jack less than a King, and so on. The Ace is a problem: sometimes it is the high card, sometimes the low card. A card would possess the characteristics suit and value. When playing card games cards are dealt from the deck into hands of some number of cards: thirteen cards for bridge, five for most poker games, and so on. The value of a card usually matters. Sometimes cards are compared against each other (poker), sometimes the sum of values is key (blackjack, cribbage), and sometimes the suit matters. These uses of a deck of cards can be used to define how classes will be created to implement card games on a computer.

Operations on a card could include to *view* it (it could be face up or face down) and to *compare* it against another card. Comparison operations could include a set of complex specifications to allow for aces being high or low and for some cards having special values (spades, baccarat) so a definition step might be very important.

A deck is a collection of cards. There is usually one of each card in a deck, but in some places (e.g., Las Vegas) there could be four or more complete decks used when playing Blackjack. Operations on a deck would include to *shuffle*, to *replace* the entire deck, and to *deal* a card or a hand. With these things in mind, a draft of some Python classes for implementing a card deck can be created:

```
class card:                      class deck:
    def __init__ (self,              def __init__ (self):
    face, suit):                     def deal_card ():
    def value():                     def deal_hand (ncards):
    def suit():                      def shuffle():
    def facevalue():                 def replace():
    def view ():
    def compare():
    def initialize()
```

The way that the methods are implemented depends on the underlying representation. When the programmer calls **deal**(), they expect the method to return a **card**, which is an instance of the card class. How that happens is not relevant to them, but it is relevant to the person who implements the class. In addition, how it happens may be different on different computers, but as long as the result is the same, it does not matter.

For example, a card could be a constant value **r** that represented one of the 52 cards in the deck. The class could contain a set of values for these cards and provide them to programmers as a reference:

```
class card:
    CLUBS_1 = 1
    DIAMONDS_1 = 2
        . . .
    HEARTS_ACE = 51
    SPADES_ACE = 52

    Def __init__ (self, face, suit):
        . . .
```

The variables CLUBS_1, DIAMONDS_1, and so on are accessible in all instances of the card class and have the appropriate value. Variables defined in this way have one instance only, and are shared by all instances.

A second implementation could be as a tuple. The ace of clubs would be (Clubs, 1), for instance. Each has advantages, but these will not be apparent to the user of the class. For example, the tuple implementation makes it easier to determine the suit of a card. This matters to games that have trump suits. The integer value implementation makes it easier to determine values and do specific comparisons. The value of a card could be stored in a tuple named **ranks**, for example, and **ranks[r]** would be a numerical value associated with the specific card.

Cat-a-Pult

Early in the development of personal computers, a simple game was created that involved shooting cannons. The player would set an angle and a power level and a cannonball would be fired towards the opposing cannon. If the ball struck the cannon, then it would be destroyed, but if not then the opposing player (or the computer) would fire back at the player's cannon. This process would continue until one or the other cannon was destroyed. This game evolved with time, having more complex graphics, mountainous terrain, and more complex aspects. Its influence can be seen in modern games like *Angry Birds*.

FIGURE 6.1 An Example of the Cannon Game.

A variation of this game is proposed as an example of how classes can be used. The basic idea is to eliminate a mouse that is eating your garden by firing cats at it; hence the name **cat-a-pult**. The game will use text as input and output, because no graphics facility is available yet. A player types the angle and the power level, and the computer will fire a cat at the mouse. The location where the cat lands will be marked on a simple character display and the player can try again. The goal is to hit the mouse with as few tries as possible.

Basic Design

Before writing any code, one needs to consider the items in this game and the actions they can take. The items will be *classes*, the actions will be *methods*. There seem to be two items: a *cannonball* (a cat) and a *cannon*. The target (the mouse) could be a class too. The cannon has a location, an angle, and a power or force with which the cannonball will be ejected. Both of the last two factors affect the distance the ball travels. The cannon is given a target as a parameter—in this example the target will be another cannon, basically to avoid making yet another class definition.

The action a cannon can perform is to be *fired*. This involves releasing a cannonball with a particular speed and direction from the location of the cannon. In this implementation an instance of the cannonball class will be created when the cannon is fired and will be given the angle and velocity as initial parameters; the ball will, from then on, be independent. As a class, the ball has a position (x,y) and a speed (dx, dy). The action that it can perform is to move, which will be accomplished using a method named **step()**, and to collide with something, accomplished by the method **testCollision()**.

Detailed Design

In the metaphor of this game, the cannonball is actually a cat and the target is a mouse, but to the program these details are not important. Here's what *is* important:

Class Cannon	Class Ball
Has:	
position x, y	position x, y
angle (when fired)	speed dx, dy
power (when fired)	name (text)
target (another cannon)	target (a Cannon class instance)

(continued)

Class Cannon	Class Ball
ball	gravity (force changing the height)
Does:	
fire	step
step	test for collision

All of the *Has* aspects are class local variables, and in this design they will be initialized within the **__init__** method of each class. This would entail the following:

self.x = x	self.x = x
self.y = y	self.y = y
self.power = 0	self.dx = dx
self.angle = 0	self.dy = dy
self.target = target	self.target = target
self.ball = None	self.gravity = 1.0
	self.name = ""

The game is essentially one-dimensional. The cannonball will land at a specific x coordinate, and if that is near enough to the x coordinate of the target, then the target is destroyed and the game is over. Without a way to draw proper graphics, this can be imagined as a simple text display with the cannon on one side of the screen and the target on the other, something like that seen in Figure 6.1.

The slash character ("/") on the left represents the cannon, and the "Y" represents the mouse, which is the target. The cannon is at horizontal coordinate 12, and the mouse is at 60; both vertical coordinates are 0.

All of the *Does* aspects represent actions, or things the class object can *do*. When the cannon is fired, the ball is created at the cannon coordinates (12, 0) and is given a speed that is related to the angle and power level using the usual trigonometric calculations learned in high school (Figure 6.2):

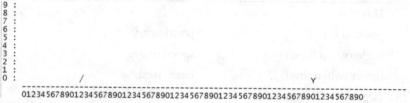

FIGURE 6.2 ASCII (text) video of the game at the beginning.

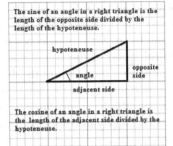 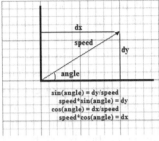

FIGURE 6.3 (Left) A review of how sines and cosines are computed. (Right) using the definition of sine and cosine to calculate the speed of the ball (or any object) in the x and y direction.

```
dy = sin(angle * 3.1415/180.0)
dx = cos(angle * 3.1415/180.0)
```

The angles passed to **sin** and **cos** must be in radians, so the value PI/180 is used to convert degrees into radians. The coordinates in this case have **y** increasing as the ball moves upwards. So, when the cannon is fired, a ball is created that has the x and y coordinates of the cannon and the **dx** and **dy** values determined as above. This is accomplished by a method named **fire()**:

Fire: takes an angle and a power.

> Angle is in degrees, between 0 and 360
>
> Power is between 0 and 100 (a percentage)

1) compute values for dx and dy from angle and power, where max power is 0.1.
2) create an instance of Ball giving it x, y, dx, dy, a name ("cat"), and a target (the mouse).

The simulation makes time steps of a fixed duration and calculates positions of objects at the end of that step. Each object should have a method that updates the time by one interval, and it will be named **step()**. The cannon does not move, but sometimes it has a cannonball that it has fired, so updating the status of the cannon should update the status of the ball as well:

Step: make one time step for this object in the simulation. No parameter.

1) If a ball has been fired, then update its position. This is done by calling the **step()** method of the ball.

> This defines the cannon.

The ball must also possess a **step**() method, and it will update the ball's position based on its current speed and location. The **x** position is increased by **dx**, and the **y** is increased by **dy**. Gravity pulls down on the ball, effectively decreasing the vertical speed of the ball at each interval. After some trials it was determined that the value of **dy** should be decreased by the value of **gravity** at each interval. If the ball strikes the ground, it should stop moving. When does this happen? When **y** becomes smaller than 0. When this occurs, set **dx** and **dy** to 0 and check to see if the impact location is near to the target.

Step: make one time step for this object in the simulation. No parameter.

1) Let x = x + dx, changing the x position.
2) Let y = y + dy, changing the y position.
3) Decrease dy by gravity (dy = dy - gravity)
4) if the ball has struck the ground
5) let dx = dy = gravity = 0
6) check for collision with target

Checking to see if the ball hit the target is a matter of looking at the x value of the ball and the x value of the target. If the difference is smaller than some predefined value, say 1.0, then the target was hit. This is determined by a method that will be called **testCollision**(). If the collision occurred then success has been achieved by the player, so set a flag that will end the game.

testCollision: check to see if the ball has hit the target; if so, set a flag.

1) subtract the x position of the ball from the x position of the target. Call this **d**.
2) if **d** <= 1.0 then set a flag **done** to **True**.

This defines the class **Ball** and completes the two major classes.

The main program that uses these classes could look something like this:

```
mouse = Cannon (60, 0, None)      # Create the target
player = Cannon (12, 0, mouse)    # create the cannon
player.fire (42, 65)    # Example: fire cannon at 42 degrees
                          65% power
done = False            # initialize variable 'done'
while not done:         # so long as the simulation is not over
    player.step()       # Update the position of the ball.
```

The previous process loosely defines a way to design and code a program that uses classes.

```
from math import *                 def testCollision (self):
class Ball:                            global done
    def __init__ (self,x, y,            d = self.xPos-
dx, dy, name, other):                      self.other.x
        self.xPos = x                  if d<0: d = -d
        self.yPos = y                  if d < 1.0:
        self.xSpeed = dx                   done = True
        self.ySpeed = dy
        self.gravity = 1.0      class Cannon:
        self.name = name            def __init__ (self, x,
        self.other = other                  y, other):
                                        self.x = x
# One time step                         self.y = y
    def step (self):                    self.other = other
        self.xPos = self.xPos           self.ball = None
+
           self.xSpeed              def fire(self,angle,power):
        self.yPos = self.yPos           dy = sin(angle*
+                                          3.1415/180.0)
           self.ySpeed              dx = cos(angle *
        self.ySpeed =                      3.1415/180.0)
           self.ySpeed-                 self.ball = Ball(self.x,
              self.gravity              self.y, dx*power/10.0,
        if self.yPos < 0:                 dy*power/10.0, "Cat",
            self.xSpeed = 0               self.other)
        self.xSpeed = 0
        self.gravity = 0           def step (self):
        self.yPos = 0                  if self.ball != None:
        self.testCollision()              (self.ball).step()
```

FIGURE 6.4 The **Ball** and the **Cannon** classes from the Cat-a-pult
simulation.

FIGURE 6.5 Frames from the text animation of the game.

Subclasses and Inheritance

Classes are designed as language features that can represent a hierarchy of information or structure. A class can be used to define another, and properties from the first class will be passed on (inherited) by the other. A class that is based on another in this way is called a *subclass*, and explanatory examples suffuse the Internet: a pet class with dogs and cats as special cases; a polygon having triangles and rectangles as subclasses;

a *dessert* class, having subclasses *pie, cake,* and *cookie*; even the initial example in this chapter of the man class and a hypothetical person class that it could be derived from. A *subclass* is a more specific case of the *superclass* (or *parent* class) on which it is based.

The examples above are for explanation, and are not really useful as software components, which begs a question about whether subclasses are really useful things. They are, but it requires non-trivial examples to really demonstrate this.

Non-Trivial Example: Objects in a Video Game

To some degree all objects in a game have some things in common. They are things that can interact with other game objects; they have a position within the volume of space defined by the game and they have a visual appearance. Thus, a description of a class that could implement a game object would include:

```
class gobject:
    position = (0, 0, 0)  # Object position in 3D
    visual = None         # Graphics that represent the object
    def __init__ (self, pos, vis)
    def getPosition (self):
    def setPosition(self, p):
    def setVisual(self, v):
    def draw (self):
```

Anyone who has played a video game knows that some of the objects can move while others cannot. Objects that move can have their position change, and it has to be updated regularly. An object that can move can have a speed and a method that updates its position; otherwise it is like a **gobject**. This is a good case for a subclass:

```
class mobject (gobject):
    speed = (0, 0, 0)  # Speed in pixels per frame the
                       # x,y,z directions
    def __init__ (self, s)
    def getSpeed(self):
    def setSpeed(self, s):
    def move(self):
    def collision(self, gobject):
```

The syntax of this has the superclass **gobject** as a parameter (apparently) of the subclass **mobject** being defined. If an instance of a **gobject** is created, its **__init__** method is called and the resulting reference has access to all of the methods in the **gobject** definition, just as one would expect. If an instance of **mobject** is created, the __init__ method of **mobject** is called, but not that of **gobject**. Nonetheless, all properties and methods of both classes are available through the **mobject** reference; that is, the following is legal:

```
m = mobject ( (12, 0, 0)) # Create mboject with speed (12,0,0)
m.draw()                  # Draw this object
```

even though an **mobject** does not possess a method **draw**(); the method defined in the parent class is accessible and will be used. When the **mobject** is created, it is also a **gobject**, and all of the variables and methods belonging to a **gobject** are defined also. However, the __init__() method for **gobject** is not called unless the **mobject** __init__() method does so. This means that, for the **mobject**, the values of **position** and **visual** are not specified by the constructor and will take the default values they were given in the **gobject** class. If no such value was given, they will be undefined and an error will occur if they are referenced.

Calling the __init__() method of the parent class can be done as follows:

```
super().__init__((10,10,10), None)
```

In this instance the constructor for **gobject** is called, passing a position and a visual. This would normally be done only in the __init__() of the subclass.

Now consider the following code. The methods are mainly stubs that print a message, but the output of the program is instructive:

```
class gobject:
# Object position in 3D
#  position = (0, 0, 0)
# Graphics that
# represent the object
  visual = None
  def __init__
     (self,pos,vis):
    self.position = pos
    self.visual = vis
    print ("gobject init")
```

```
class mobject (gobject):
# Speed in pixels per frame
# the x,y,z directions
  speed = (0, 0, 0)
  def __init__ (self, s):
    self.speed = s
    super().__init__
       ((10,10,10), None)
    print ("mobject init")

  def getSpeed(self):
    print ("getSpeed")
```

(continued)

```
def getPosition(self):              return self.speed
    return self.position        def setSpeed(self, s):
    print                           print ("setSpeed")
        ("getPosition")             self.speed = s
def setPosition(self,           def move(self):
            p):                     print ("Move")
    self.position = p           def collision(self,
    print                               gobject):
        ("setPosition")             print ("collision")
def setVisual(self,
            v):                 g = gobject ((12, 12,12), None)
    self.visual = v             m = mobject((13,13,13))
    print ("setVisual")         print (m.getPosition())
def draw (self):                m.move()
    print("Draw")               m.draw()
```

Output from this is:

gobject init	from the creation of the gobject instance g
gobject init	when m is created it calls the parent __init__
mobject init	from the mobject __init__ when m is created
(10, 10, 10)	m.getPosition, showing access to parent methods
Move	m.move call
Draw	m.draw call, again showing access to parent method

Attempting to call **g.move()** would fail because there is no **move()** method within the **gobject** class. Hence if an object was passed to a function that would attempt to move it, it would be critical to know whether the parameter passed was a **gobject** or an **mobject**. Consider a method that moves an object **x** out of the path of an **mobject** instance if it can, or changes the path of the **mobject** if it cannot. This method, named **dodge()**, might do the following:

```
def dodge self, (x):
    c = x.getPosition()
    c = c + (dx, dy, 0)
    x.setPosition (c)
```

However, if the parameter is an instance of a **gobject**, then it should not be moved. The function **isinstance()** can be used to determine this. The result of:

```
isinstance (x, gobject)
```

will be **True** if x is a **gobject** and **False** otherwise. If **False** then it can't be moved and the **dodge()** method will have to move the current **mobject** out of the way instead:

```
def dodge self, (x):
    if isinstance(x, gobject):
        self.position = self.position + (dx, dy, 0)
else:
    c = x.getPosition()
    c = c + (dx, dy, 0)
    x.setPosition (c)
```

Duck Typing

In many programming languages types are immutable and compatibility is enforced. This is not generally true in Python, but still there are operations that require specific types. Indexing into a string or tuple must be done using something much like an integer, and not by using a float. Now that classes can be used to build what amounts to new types, more attention should be paid to the things a type should offer and the requirements this puts on a programmer. A Python philosophy could be that the fewer restrictions the better, and this is a principle of *duck typing* as well.

It should not really matter what the exact type of the object is that is being manipulated, only that it possesses the properties that are needed. In a very simple case, consider the classes point and triangle that were discussed at the beginning of this chapter. It was proposed that both could have a **draw**() method that would create a graphical representation of these on the screen, and both have a **move**() method as well. A function could be written that would move a *triangle* away from a *point* and draw them both:

```
def moveaway (a, b)
    dx = a.getx()-b.getx()
    dy = a.gety()-d.gety()
    a.move (dx/10, dy/10)
    b.move (-dx/10, -dy/10)
```

Question: which of the parameters, **a** or **b**, is the *triangle*, and which is the *point*? Answer: it does not matter. Both classes have the methods needed by this function, namely **getx**(), **gety**(), and **move**(). Because of this the calls are symmetrical, and both of the following are the same:

```
moveaway (a, b)
moveaway (b, a)
```

In fact, any class that possesses these three methods can be passed to **moveaway**() and a result will be calculated without error. The essence of duck typing is that, so long as an object offers the service needed (i.e., a method of the correct name and parameter set) to another function or method, then the call is acceptable. There is a way to tell whether the class instance **a** has a **getx()** method. The built-in function **hasattr()**:

```
if hasattr (v1, "getx"):
    x = v1.getx()
```

The first argument is a class instance and the second is the name of the method that is needed, as a string. It returns **True** if the method exists.

The name comes from the old saying that "if something walks like a duck and quacks like a duck, then it *is* a duck." As long as a class offers the things asked for, then it can be used in that context.

GRAPHICS, MEDIA, AND INTERFACES

A t the most primitive level of graphics software is the ability to set individual pixels. It is quite difficult to use this capability to create complex pictures. How is a dog drawn, or a building, or even just a straight line? Fortunately, those things have been figured out.

At the bottom layer of software are functions that manipulate *pixels*. At the next level are *lines* and *curves*; these are the basic components of drawings and sketches. An artist with a pencil uses lines and curves to represent scenes. At the level above lines are functions that use lines to create other objects, such as *rectangles, circles,* and *ellipses*. These can be line drawings or can be filled with colors. The next higher levels can be argued about, but *text* is probably in the next software layer and then shading and images followed by 3D objects, which includes perspective transformation and textures.

Python itself does not have graphics tools, but various modules that are associated with Python do. The standard graphical user interface library for use with Python is *tkinter*. There are many features of this module, including the creation of windows, drawing, user interface widgets such as buttons, and a host of other features. It is free and is normally included in the Python distribution.

Another library that allows graphics programming is called *Pygame*, and this is designed for building computer games using Python. Let's look in detail at *Pygame*, as it will allow us to draw pictures, manage interfaces, and do animations.

Installing Pygame

Download Pygame for Windows from:

http://pygame.org/ftp/pygame-1.9.1.win32-py2.7.msi

Apple:

http://pygame.org/ftp/pygame-1.9.1release-py2.6-macosx10.5.zip

Ubuntu Linux users can type `sudo apt-get install python-pygame`. Other Linux and Unix distributions can be downloaded through *http://www. pygame.org/download.shtml*

And follow the installation notes at:

http://www.pygame.org/wiki/GettingStarted

Essentials: The Graphics Window and Colors

To start creating computer graphics, it is necessary to understand how Pygame manages the screen and other resources. There is a distinct set of steps that must be followed in order for even the simplest Pygame program to work. After the basic steps are accomplished, we can draw into a graphics window and have it appear on the screen.

The first step is to import the Pygame library. Assuming that it has been installed correctly, this is a matter of beginning with the statement:

```
import pygame
```

FIGURE 7.1 The Pygame Window.

Next, there are variables that need to be initialized and storage that has to be allocated for Pygame to work. One example is that fonts must be loaded and placed into a data structure. This is done with the statement:

```
pygame.init()
```

Nothing seems to happen, but Pygame is now ready to work. Next we create a drawing structure called a *surface*:

```
surf = pygame.display.set_
mode((400, 450))
```

This surface will be 400 pixels wide by 450 pixels high, and will appear briefly on the screen and will then vanish. Why vanish? Because the program ends after the last statement taking the window with it.

The variable **surf** will contain a reference to a surface object, and in this case it will be the *display surface*, because we accessed it through the display part of the pygame object. The display surface is the place where things are drawn if we want them to be visible on the screen. There are other surfaces that can be drawn on that will not display by default. The method *set_mode* takes a tuple as a parameter that gives the size of the surface.

How can we keep the drawing area on the screen? Don't end the program until told! We could, as one example, read something from the keyboard and then terminate the program. Here's the first full Pygame program, which is nonstandard but functional:

```
import pygame
pygame.init()
surf = pygame.display.set_mode((400, 400))
pygame.display.update()
input()
```

The window will stay on the screen until a character is typed in the input region (not the drawing window!)

Simple Static Drawing

Everything drawn on the display surface has a color, and it is a tuple consisting of the red, green, and blue component of the color. Thus, the tuple (255,255,255) can be a color, and would be white. (0,0,0) would be black. To humans, colors have names. Here's a list of some named colors and their RGB equivalents:

Color	Red	Green	Blue	Color	Red	Green	Blue
Black	0	0	0	Olive	128	128	0
White	255	255	255	Khaki	240	230	140
Red	255	0	0	Teal	0	128	128
Green	0	255	0	Sienna	160	83	45
Blue	0	0	255	Tan	210	180	140
Yellow	255	255	0	Indigo	75	0	130
Magenta	255	0	255	Orange	255	165	0

The background is black by default. Assuming that the display surface is named **surf**, then the background color can be changed by a call to the fill method, passing a tuple specifying the color:

```
surf.fill ((255, 0, 0))
```

In this case the background color will be red. Pygame also has a *Color* class that has red, green, and blue components and methods for converting to non-RGB color specifications like HSV. After:

```
c = pygame.Color(255,0,0)
surf.fill (c)
```

the color stored in **c** will be red as will the background color.

Pixel-Level Graphics

The only pixel-level operation draws a pixel at a specified location; so, for example, the call:

```
surf.set_at ((x, y), c)
```

will set the pixel at coordinates (**x,y**) to the color **c**. Setting a collection of pixels that are adjacent to each other will create a line.

Example: Create a Page of Notepaper

Notepaper has blue lines separated by enough space to write or print text between them. It often has a red vertical line indicating an indentation level, a place to begin writing. Drawing this is a matter of drawing a set of connected blue pixels in vertically separated rows, and **then making a vertical column of red pixels. Here is one way to code this:**

```
import pygame
pygame.init()
surf = pygame.display.set_
mode((400, 400))
```

FIGURE 7.2 A graphic of a sheet of lined paper.

```
c = pygame.Color(0,0,200)
surf.fill ((255,255,255))
y = 60                          # Height at which to start
for n in range (0, 27):         # Draw 30 horizontal blue lines
    for x in range (0,400):     # Draw all pixels in one line
        surf.set_at ((x, y),c)  # Draw a blue pixel
    y = y + 20                  # The next line is 20 pixels down
c = (200, 0, 0)                 # Pixel color red
for y in range (0, 400):        # Draw connected vertical pixels
    surf.set_at ((25, y), c)    #  to form the margin line
pygame.display.update()
input()
```

The output of this program is shown in Figure 7.2. When pixels are drawn immediately next to each other they appear to be connected, and so in this case they form horizontal and vertical lines. This is not easy to do for arbitrary lines; it is not obvious exactly which pixels to fill for a line between, say, (10, 20) and (99, 17). That's why the line-drawing functions exist.

Example: Creating a Color Gradient

When creating a visual on a computer, the first step is to have a clear picture of what it will look like. For this example, imagine the sky on a clear day. The horizon shows a lighter blue than the sky directly above, and the color changes continuously all the way from horizon to zenith. If a realistic sky background were needed, then it would be necessary to draw this using the tools available. What would the method be?

First, decide on what the color is at the horizon (y=ymax) and at the highest point in the scene (y=ymin). Now ask: "how many pixels between those points?" The change in pixel color will be the color difference from ymax to ymin divided by the number of pixels. Now simply draw rows of pixels beginning with the horizon and moving up the image (i.e., decreasing Y value), changing the color by this amount each time.

As an implementation, assume that the color at the horizon will be blue = (40, 40, 255) and the top of the image will be (40, 40, 128), a darker blue. The height of the image will be 400 pixels; the change in blue over that range is 127 units. Thus, the color change over each pixel is going to be 255.0/400. A color can't change a fractional amount, of course, but what this means is that the blue value will decrease by approximately 1 unit for the increase in height of every couple of pixels. Do not forget that the horizon is at the bottom of the image, which has the greatest Y coordinate value, so that an increase in Y means a decrease in height and vice versa.

The example program that implements this is:

```
import pygame
pygame.init()
surf = pygame.display.set_
mode((400, 400))
surf.fill ((255,255,255))
blue = 0
delta = 255.0/400
for y in range (0, 400):
    yy = 400-y
    c = (40, 40, blue)
    for x in range(0, 400):
        surf.set_at ((x,
y), c)
    blue = blue + delta
pygame.display.update()
input()
```

FIGURE 7.3. A color gradient drawn as pixels.

Figure 7.3 shows what the gradient image looks like in greys.

Lines and Curves

Straight lines and curves are more complex objects than pixels, consisting of many pixels in an organized arrangement. A line is actually drawn by setting pixels, though. The fact that a **line()** function exists means that the programmer does not have to figure out what pixels to draw and can focus on the higher level construct, the line or curve.

A line is drawn by specifying the endpoints of the line. Using *Pygame* the call is:

```
pygame.draw.line ( surf, col, (x0, y0), (x1, y1))
```

where one end of the line is at (x0,y0) and the other is at (x1,y1). The color of the line is specified by the second parameter **col**. If any part of the line extends past the boundary of the window that's OK; the line will be clipped to fit.

Example: Notepaper Again

The example of drawing a piece of notepaper can be done using lines instead of pixels, and will be a lot faster. Draw a collection of horizontal lines (i.e., that have the same Y coordinate at the endpoints) separated by 20 pixels, as before having a blue color. Then draw a vertical red line for the margin. The program is a variation on the previous version:

```
import pygame

pygame.init()
y = 60                          # Height at which to start
width = 400
height = 400
surf = pygame.display.set_mode((width, height),pygame.SRCALPHA)
surf.fill ((255,255,255))
y = 60                          # Height at which to start
for n in range (0, 27):    # Draw 30 horizontal blue lines
    pygame.draw.line (surf, (0,0,200), (0, y), (width, y))
    y = y + 20                  # The next line is 20 pixels down
c = (200, 0, 0)                 # Pixel color red
pygame.draw.line (surf, c, (25,0), (25,height))
pygame.display.update()
input()
```

The output from this program is the same as that for the version that drew pixels, which is shown in Figure 7.2.

A *curve* is trickier than a line, in that it is harder to specify. The method used in Pygame is common: a curve (arc) is defined as a portion of an ellipse from a starting angle for a specified number of degrees, as referenced from the center of the ellipse. Here's a call to **arc**:

pygame.draw.arc (surf, c, box, start_angle, end_angle)

The parameter **surf** is the surface to draw on, **c** is the color, **box** is an enclosing bounding box as a tuple (upper left x, upper left Y, width, height), **start _angle** is an angle between 0 and 2π radians, and **stop_ angle** is an angle in the same range. The angle 0 is to the right, 90 degrees is up, 180 degree (π radians) is left, and 270 degrees is down. The angle specifies the part of the ellipse to draw. So:

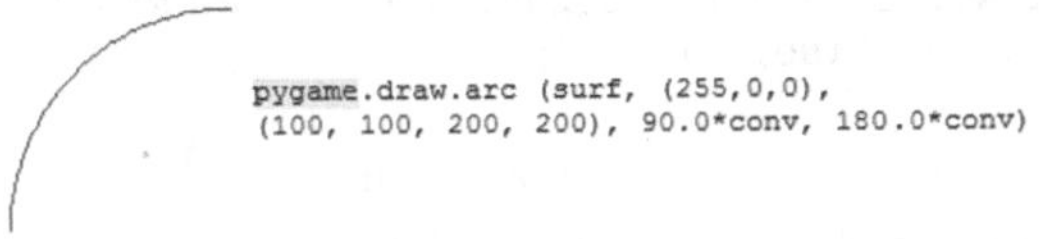

```
pygame.draw.arc (surf, (255,0,0),
(100, 100, 200, 200), 90.0*conv, 180.0*conv)
```

FIGURE 7.4 ARC example 1.

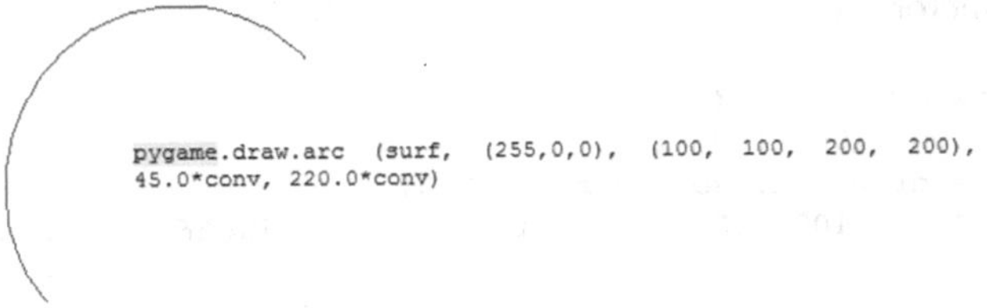

```
pygame.draw.arc (surf, (255,0,0), (100, 100, 200, 200),
45.0*conv, 220.0*conv)
```

FIGURE 7.5 ARC example 2.

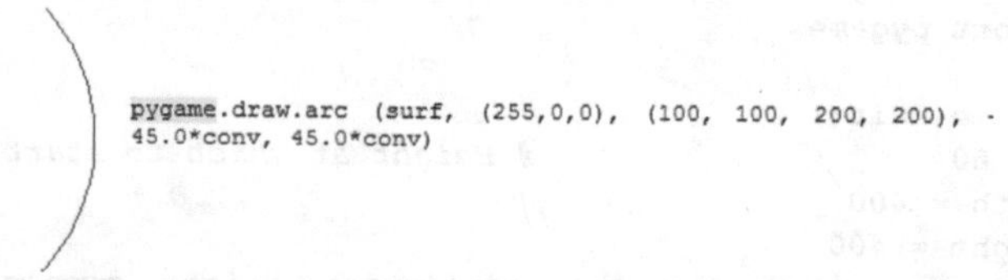

```
pygame.draw.arc (surf, (255,0,0), (100, 100, 200, 200), ·
45.0*conv, 45.0*conv)
```

FIGURE 7.6 ARC example 3.

The curves are drawn counterclockwise. The value **conv** is π/180, and converts an angle in degrees into radians when multiplied.

Polygons

For the purposes of discussion, a polygon will include all closed regions, including ellipses and circles.

A rectangle is drawn using the **rect** method.

```
Pygame.draw.rect (surf, ((0,200,
50), (100, 100, 200, 300))
```

FIGURE 7.7 Filled rectangle.

The **surf** and **color** parameters are as before, and the **box** is specified as the upper left coordinates, the width, and the height. By default the rectangle is filled with the specified color.

An additional final argument specifies the line thickness with which to draw the rectangle, and if this is specified then the rectangle is not filled with color:

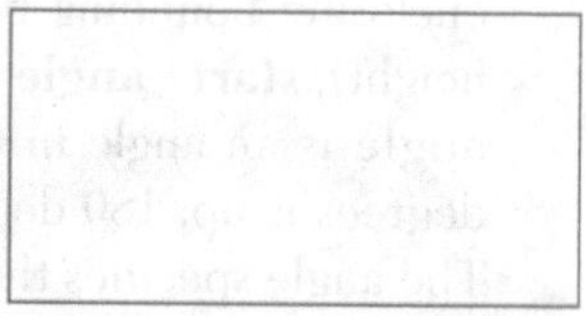

FIGURE 7.8 Unfilled rectangle.

```
pygame.draw.rect (surf, (0,200, 50),
(100, 100, 200, 100), 1)
```

The **ellipse** method takes the same parameters as does **rect**, and draws an ellipse within the rectangle defined by the third parameter.

```
pygame.draw.rect (surf, (230,230,
0), (100, 100, 200, 100), 1)
pygame.draw.ellipse (surf, (0,200,
50), (100, 100, 200, 100), 1)
```

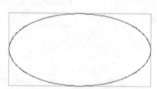

FIGURE 7.9 Unfilled ellipse.

A circle is an ellipse drawn in a square. This makes the center and radius rather implicit. There is a **circle** method also:

```
pygame.draw.rect (surf, (230,230, 0),
(50, 50, 100, 100), 1)
pygame.draw.circle (surf, (0,200, 50),
(100, 100), 50)
```

FIGURE 7.10. Filled circle.

The third parameter to a circle is a tuple defining the center, and the fourth is the radius. A fifth would be the line thickness, and filling would turn off. In the case here of a circle at (100,100) and a radius of 50, the enclosing square would be from (100-50, 100-50), which is (50, 50), for (100,100) pixels.

Blitting

To *blit* is to combine several graphics or bitmaps into a single one. It is often accomplished using a Boolean function, and often is very fast due to hardware assistance. Pygame has one special Surface that is the display Surface, but allows us to draw on other surfaces too. To display what is drawn on these surfaces we would *blit* them to the display Surface.

Blitting has consequences and requires specifications that are not usually appreciated by the definition. Consider the creation of two Surfaces named **s1** and **s2** in addition to the display surface, and drawing into each of those:

```
s1 = pygame.Surface((400,400)) # New Surface
pygame.draw.rect (s1, (230,230, 0), (50, 50, 100, 100), 1)
s2 = pygame.Surface((400,400)) # New Surface
pygame.draw.circle (s2, (0,200, 50), (100, 100), 50)
```

The Surface **s1** contains a rectangle, and the Surface **s2** contains a circle. Neither appears on the display Surface, which as usual is named **surf**. A blit is a copy from one Surface to another. Some questions are:

- Which part of the Surface being blitted is copied?
- Where (coordinates) is the surface being blitted to?
- What happens to the pixels that already exist in the region being blitted to?

The method that copies (blits) one surface to another is *blit*, the simplest form of which is:

```
surf.blit (s1, (0,0))
```

This copies all of Surface **s1** to **surf** so that the upper left of **s1** is at (0,0) of **surf**. We can copy **s1** to any pixel coordinate in **surf**. To draw a circle and a rectangle in different Surfaces and then blit them to the display Surface would involve creating the surfaces, drawing in them, and blitting them:

```
s1 = pygame.Surface((200,200))      # S1 is 200x200
s1.fill ((255,255,255))             # White background
pygame.draw.rect (s1, (230,230, 0), (50, 50, 100, 100), 1)
s2 = pygame.Surface((200,200))      # s2 is also 200x200 pixels
s2.fill ((255,255,255))             # White background too
pygame.draw.circle (s2, (0,200, 50), (60, 60), 50)

# Blit rectangle to (0,0) and circle to (100,100)
surf.blit (s1, (0,0))               # s1 has a rectangle: blit
surf.blit (s2, (100,100))           # s2 has a circle: blit
pygame.display.update()
```

Here **s1** is blitted before **s2** (i.e., is drawn first), and there is overlap between the drawn regions. Thus, the one drawn last (**s2**) appears to be drawn *over* **s1**. If we think in terms of layers, the last surface drawn is the top layer, and is visible. Layers beneath may be partly or completely covered by layers above. A Surface is rectangular, so notice that the background surrounding the circle is also drawn over the square below.

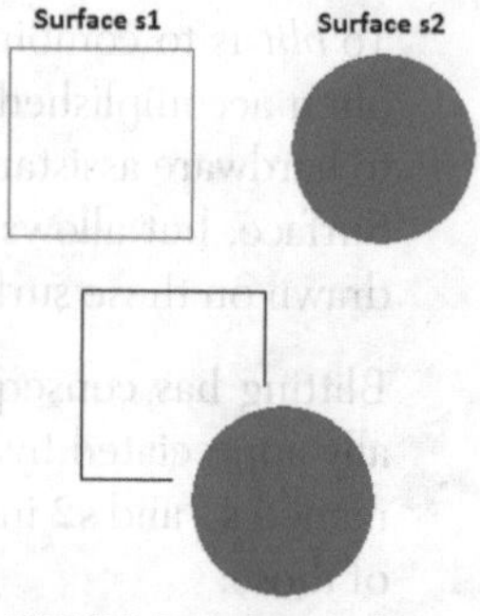

The blit function has other parameters that we'll get into shortly.

FIGURE 7.11 One surface blitted to another.

Drawing Text

Drawing text is accomplished by loading a font and then drawing (rendering) a text string to a surface using that font as a guide. An instance of the Font class, and there is a default for that, can render text onto a surface. That surface is then blitted to the target surface, possibly the display. A simple example involves placing the text "Hello there" at location (100,100):

```
pygame.init()               # Must initialize pygame and fonts
font = pygame.font.Font(None, 36)
text = font.render("Hello There", 1, (10, 10, 10))
surf.blit (text, (100,100))
```

The method **pygame.font.Font** selects a font to be used and returns an instance. A font has a name, in this case **None** indicating that we should use the default, and a size, in this case 36. Each computer system has a different set of fonts available, so we'll use the default. Next, the font class can draw (render) the text onto a surface. The call:

```
text = font.render("Hello There", 1, (0,0,255))
```

renders the text "Hello there" in the color (0,0,255), which is blue. The second parameter 1 means to anti-alias, which will yield nice smooth characters. Finally:

```
surf.blit (text, (100,100))
```

will blit the text to the display Surface **surf** at location (100,100). The coordinates (100,100) are those of the upper left of the text Surface, which will be a rectangle large enough to enclose the string.

Hello There

FIGURE 7.12 Rendering text.

A problem is that this text Surface will write over anything underneath as a rectangular area. This can be fixed by using a transparent background.

Transparent Colors

When one pixel is drawn over the top of (i.e., at the same location as) another, the one drawn most recently will be visible. This may not always be what is needed. Background pixels of text images being blitted should be invisible so that the background can be seen with the text on top.

Transparency is a value that can be numerical. Let's say that a value of 0 means that the drawn pixel is invisible and a value of 255 means that it is opaque. Values in between have degrees of transparency. Then we want the background of a text box to have a value of this parameter of 0, and the text to have a value of 255. Looking at this value it has the same properties as does a colour component, and so it is generally implemented as a fourth component called *alpha*. A color can be specified as RGBA, which means four components: red, green, blue, and alpha.

Not all Surface objects can implement transparency. They must have a property called 32-bit color and have the **SCRALPHA** property. Creating a Surface like this is done as follows:

```
surf = pygame.display.set_mode((w, h), pygame.SRCALPHA, 32)
```

where the third parameter means that the Surface can support transparency and the final one means that it has 32-bit colors: 4 values of 8 bits each.

The previous example having a rectangle and a circle drawn and then blitted to the display Surface can now be implemented using transparency:

FIGURE 7.13 Surface with transparent background (circle) blitted to another.

```
surf = pygame.display.set_mode((400, 400), pygame.SRCALPHA)
surf.fill ((255,255,255))
s1 = pygame.Surface((200,200), pygame.SRCALPHA, 32)
s1 = s1.convert_alpha()
s1.fill ((255,255,255, 0))
pygame.draw.rect (s1, (230,230, 0), (50, 50, 100, 100), 1)
s2 = pygame.Surface((200,200), pygame.SRCALPHA, 32)
s2 = s2.convert_alpha()
s2.fill ((255,255,255, 0))
pygame.draw.circle (s2, (0,200, 50), (60, 60), 50)
surf.blit (s1, (0,0))
surf.blit (s2, (100,100))
pygame.display.update()
input()
```

The fill color value of (255,255,255,0) yields a fully transparent color that will comprise the background of the circle and the rectangle Surface, allowing the background to show through.

Images

Unlike the graphical components displayed so far, an *image* is fundamentally a collection of pixels. A camera captures an image and stores it digitally as pixels, and so it was never anything else. Displaying an image means drawing each pixel in the appropriate color, as captured. *Pygame* can load and display images in files of various formats: JPEG, GIF, BMP, and PNG.

FIGURE 7.14 The original "Checkpoint Charlie" image.

Unlike languages such a Java, Python has no image class. An image is read from a file using the function **pygame.image.load** and is returned as a Surface. This means that it can be displayed immediately using a blit and that individual pixels can be accessed using the Surface method **get_at()**.

The file "charlie.gif" is a photo of checkpoint Charlie in Berlin (Figure 7.14). It could be read in to a Python program with the call:

```
im = pygame.image.load ("charlie.gif")
```

The variable **im** now holds the image and can be displayed using:

```
surf.blit (im, (0,0))
```

While the details are not completely relevant, it is good to know that **im.get_width()** and **im.get_height()** give the width and height of the image in pixels.

The complete Python program (using *Pygame*) that can load and display the image is thus:

```
import pygame
pygame.init()

im = pygame.image.load ("charlie.gif")
width = im.get_width()
height = im.get_height()
surf = pygame.display.set_mode((width, height),
                        pygame.SRCALPHA)
surf.fill ((255,255,255))

surf.blit (im, (0,0))
pygame.display.update()
input()
```

This displays the image in a window that is exactly the correct size.

Pixels

An image, as has been mentioned, is just a Surface after being read. Individual pixels can be accessed using the method **get_at** passing the **x** and **y** coordinates. The code

```
pix = im.get_at ((i,j))   # Parameter is a tuple
```

returns the color of the pixels at (i,j), which is a tuple containing red, green, blue, and alpha components.

Setting the value of the pixel at location (x,y) is accomplished by calling im.set_at().

```
im.set_at ((x,y), color)
```

where again, color is a tuple.

Example: Thresholding

Thresholding is an early step in many image analysis processes. It is the creation of a bi-level image, having just black and white pixels, from a grey or color image. In thresholding a simple grey value T, the *threshold*, is used to separate pixels into black and white: all pixels having a value smaller that T will be black, and the others will be white.

FIGURE 7.15 Thresholded "Checkpoint Charlie" image.

Using the Checkpoint Charlie image again, let's create a thresholded image using a threshold of 128, the middle of the possible range. First we have to convert the color pixels into grey values. An easy way to do this is to average the R, G, and B values. For a pixel value **pix**:

grey = (pix[0]+pix[1]+pix[2])/3

Now if this value is smaller than the threshold 128, the corresponding pixel in the image is set to black, or (0,0,0); otherwise it is set to white, or (255,255,255). A program that does this is:

```
import pygame
pygame.init()

im = pygame.image.load ("charlie.gif")
width = im.get_width()
height = im.get_height()

for i in range (0,width):
    for j in range(0,height):
        pix = im.get_at ((i,j))
        grey = (pix[0]+pix[1]+pix[2])/3
        if grey < 128:
            im.set_at ((i,j), (0,0,0))
```

```
    else:
        im.set_at ((i,j), (255,255,255))

surf = pygame.display.set_mode((width, height), pygame.
SRCALPHA)
surf.blit (im, (0,0))
pygame.display.update()
input()
```

Interaction

The code written so far generates and displays a single image and then waits for the user to dismiss it with a keystroke. This is a simplification of how *Pygame* usually works. Because *Pygame* was developed so that computer games could be written in Python, it must permit animation, which means it can display a new image or frame every fraction of a second. Consider a ball represented by a circle at the location (10,10) on a surface. If the ball is supposed to be moving, then the coordinates will change and it will be drawn again, this time at the new position, say (10,12). It will be drawn again at (10,14), and so on until it disappears off of the bottom of the display. This is how animation works: by the rapid display of images that incorporate the frame-by-frame changes because of motion.

But how do we display a sequence of images rather than just a single one? The call to **input()** at the end of the program prevents it from terminating, and allows the final image to stay on the screen. To display an animation we would need to display an image, wait for a fraction of a second, and then display another one, over and over. This is actually how *Pygame* was intended to be used.

In principle a loop could be used to do this. Instead of the call to **input()**, code a loop that includes changes to the graphic rendered in the Surface and then update the display surface. Here's an example, which will draw a blue circle that moves from the left to the right side of the screen:

```
import pygame
pygame.init()
x = 0
y = 100
surf = pygame.display.set_mode((400, 400), pygame.SRCALPHA)
while True:
    surf.fill ((255,255,255))
    pygame.draw.circle (surf, (0,0,200), (x,y), 20)
    x = x + 1
    pygame.display.update()
```

This is an infinite loop, and this particular one is not a recommended solution. Each time through this loop, the position of the circle is changed and the display Surface is updated, which is to say it is drawn to the screen. There is no gentle way to terminate the program, and the speed is hard to manage as well. There is a standard *Pygame* main loop used by most games that shows how the *Surface* is to be managed. It consists of an infinite loop that can control the time between iterations and can deal with user interactions between frames.

Time

A typical 32-mm film displays a new image 24 times per second. A television does so 30 times per second. Pygame allows the control of duration using a *time* module and the *Clock* class. Create an instance:

```
clock = pygame.time.Clock()
```

This class has a **tick** method. The call:

```
t = tick()
```

will return the number of milliseconds that have passed since the last time tick was called. Better yet, the call:

```
tick(30)
```

will not return until 1/30 of a second has passed since the last time tick was called. This allows us to run the loop at a standard rate:

```
clock = pygame.time.Clock()
while True:
    clock.tick(30)                # Frame rate is 30 per second
    surf.fill ((255,255,255))
    pygame.draw.circle (surf, (0,0,200), (x,y), 20)
    x = x + 1
    pygame.display.update()
```

Running this program shows the blue circle moving at a more sedate speed across the screen, moving 30 pixels each second.

Events

The best definition for an event is "something that happened." Some events can be predicted, such as when the blue circle reaches the right side of the screen. That time can be computed. Other events cannot: a key press by the user can't be predicted, nor can a mouse gesture. When using **clock.tick(30)** to control the speed of the program, it's possible that a user could press a key or two or move the mouse between interactions of the loop. *Pygame* keeps track of these events and remembers them for use, and they can be dealt with at the beginning of each loop.

The function **pygame.event.get**() will return a representation of a *Pygame* event that happened; in fact it will be the oldest one that has not been looked at. There may be more than one event that has not been looked at, so the function should be called for all recalled events:

```
for event in pygame.event.get():
```

Each time through this loop, the variable event will be an event that needs to be dealt with. Events can be:

QUIT	Program complete
KEYDOWN	Key was pressed
KEYUP	Key was released
MOUSEMOTION	The mouse has been moved
MOUSEBUTTONUP	A mouse button is released
MOUSEBUTTONDOWN	A mouse button is pressed

There are others, but these are the big six. Let's look at these events as they will actually be used.

The Mouse

The mouse is used to identify components on the display surface that the user would like to manipulate in some way. In addition to the three mouse events listed above, the mouse has a location, which is the position of the mouse cursor in the display window. The method **mouse.get_pos**() will return a tuple that has the x and y components of the mouse position. For example, the following program will draw a blue circle at the current mouse position:

```
import pygame
pygame.init()
clock = pygame.time.Clock()

surf = pygame.display.set_mode((400, 400), pygame.SRCALPHA)
while True:
    clock.tick(30)
    for event in pygame.event.get():
        pass

    surf.fill ((255,255,255))
    pygame.draw.circle (surf, (0,0,200),
                        pygame.mouse.get_pos(), 20)
    pygame.display.update()
```

Here the position of the circle, a tuple at the third parameter of the **circle** call, is the position of the mouse. This works fine. The check for events seems to not do anything here, but must be present for the program to work properly; otherwise the circle is drawn at one position and nothing else happens.

A mouse click or button press is an event, and can be identified in the **for** loop. The main issue when a mouse button press or release is determined is the location of the mouse when that happens. A release when the cursor is inside of a specific rectangle could be a *button press*, for example.

Button

Consider a rectangle at location (100,100) that is 100x30 pixels in size. When the mouse button is released while inside of this region, something will happen—the background color of the display Surface will change. This represents a button in the general sense of a computer user interface, and works in the same way.

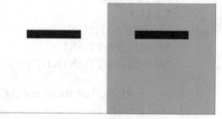

FIGURE 7.16 Button example; changing background color.

The program begins as usual, but the **for** loop has something in it: it tests the mouse position when a button-release event is detected, and if that position lies within the selected area, the background color is changed by modifying the red component, toggling it between 0 and 255.

```
import pygame
pygame.init()
clock = pygame.time.Clock()
red = 255
surf = pygame.display.set_mode((400, 400), pygame.SRCALPHA)
while True:
    clock.tick(30)
    for event in pygame.event.get():
        if event.type == pygame.MOUSEBUTTONUP:
            p = pygame.mouse.get_pos()
            if p[0]>100 and p[0]<200
                and p[1]>100 and p[1]<130:
                red = 255-red
    surf.fill ((red,255,255))
    pygame.draw.rect (surf, (0,0,200), (100,100,200,30))
    pygame.display.update()
```

Stretchy Lines

The problem is this: draw a line between two points. The first click of the mouse defines the starting point of the line, and the second click defines the end. The second point will follow the mouse until the second click occurs. The event managing the loop now looks for two events. When the MOUSEBUTTONDOWN event happens, the mouse position is used to define the point (x0,y0). When MOUSEBUTTONUP occurs then the position (x1,y1) is defined. A

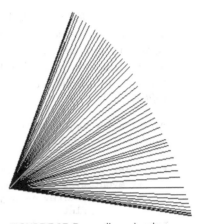

FIGURE 7.17 Draw a line using the mouse.

line is drawn between these two points. If x0 = -1 then it has not been defined, and nothing is drawn. If x1 = -1 then a line is drawn between (x0,y0) and the current mouse position.

```
Import pygame
pygame.init()
clock = pygame.time.Clock()
x0,y0 = -1,-1
x1,y1 = -1,-1
surf = pygame.display.set_mode((400, 400), pygame.SRCALPHA)
while True:
    clock.tick(30)
    p = pygame.mouse.get_pos()
    for event in pygame.event.get():
        if event.type == pygame.MOUSEBUTTONUP:
            x1,y1 = p[0],p[1]
        if event.type == pygame.MOUSEBUTTONDOWN:
            x0,y0 = p[0],p[1]
    surf.fill ((255,255,255))
    if x1 >= 0:
        pygame.draw.line (surf, (0,0,200), (x0,y0),(x1,y1))
    elif x0 >= 0:
        pygame.draw.line (surf, (0,0,200), (x0,y0),(p[0],p[1]))
    pygame.display.update()
```

The Keyboard

Keyboard events are limited to KEYDOWN and KEYUP, but there are a variety of keys that might have been pressed. When a keyboard event occurs, there is an accompanying variable key that is part of the event that indicates what key is involved. Keys all have special named constants: the letter "A" is KEY_A, for example. The critical keys for games and interaction would be the arrow keys K_LEFT, K_RIGHT, K_UP, and K_DOWN, the equivalent keys as characters K_w, K_a, K_s, and K_d, and the space key K_SPACE. These are frequently used in games. A list of characters is available *at http://www.pygame.org/docs/ref/key.html*.

An event **for** loop that would detect the up arrow key being pressed would be:

```
for event in pygame.event.get():
    if event.type == pygame.KEYDOWN:
        if event.key == pygame.K_UP:
            print ("Up arrow")
pygame.display.update()
```

Sound

Sound is complicated in *Pygame*. *Pygame* has a *mixer* class that provides much of the functionality, allowing files to be read in, multiple channels to be mixed together and played, volume control, and so on. It would be a whole chapter, so the basics are as follows. When a sound file is to be played:

1) Import pygame.mixer and initialize it.

```
import pygame.mixer
pygame.mixer.init()
```

2) Read the sound file into a variable.

```
sound = pygame.mixer.Sound ("sound.wav")
```

3) Play the sound.
```
sound.play()
```

Other aspects like mixing will not be discussed. A program that will do this is:

```
import pygame
import pygame.mixer

pygame.init()
pygame.mixer.init()
clock = pygame.time.Clock()
sound = pygame.mixer.Sound ("sound.wav")
```

```
sound.play()
surf = pygame.display.set_mode((400, 400), pygame.SRCALPHA)
surf.fill ((255,255,255))

while True:
    clock.tick(30)
        . . .
```

A sound file has to be in WAV format, but this may change in later versions of Pygame. Pygame can also play video files. See *http://www.pygame.org/docs/ref/movie.html* for details.

A Game

Because Pygame was designed to help create games, it only seems reasonable to use a game as a final example. It will have to be simple to fit in the available space, and it should use as much of the functionality that we have learned as is possible. Such a simple game is Lunar Lander, a 1970s arcade game that has the player attempting to land a spacecraft on the moon.

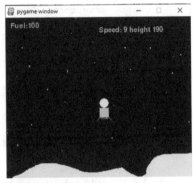

FIGURE 7.18 The Lunar Lander game.

The game begins with the craft near the top of the screen. It immediately begins to fall to the surface, which is near the bottom of the screen. Pressing the UP key powers the engines and slows the craft's fall, but also uses fuel. LEFT and RIGHT keys cause the craft to move left and right, and also use fuel. If the craft touches the ground slowly enough, then a successful landing occurs. Otherwise not.

The controls are UP, LEFT, and RIGHT. The object in the game being controlled is a lunar lander, and the background is a lunar landscape, seen in profile. The small number of objects make the game easier to implement than some others.

The Lander

The lander graphic is intended to be a low-resolution rendering of the NASA lander. The graphic origin of this drawing is the upper left corner of the grey rectangle representing the body. There is a circle above and landing legs below. The two small extensions to the landing legs are not drawn in the game but represent landing sensors. When they touch the ground the craft has landed, or it has at least touched the ground.

The lander will be drawn by a function that takes as the (x,y) parameters the location of the origin in the drawing area.

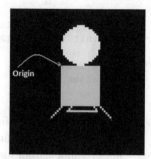

FIGURE 7.19 The Lander graphic.

```
def draw_lander (x, y):
    global power
    pygame.draw.rect   (surf,(200,200,200),(x, y,20, 20))
    pygame.draw.circle(surf,(250,250,90),(x+10,y-10), 10)
    pygame.draw.line   (surf,(200,200,200),
                             (x+5,y+20), (x+3,y+22))
    pygame.draw.line   (surf,(200,200,200),
                             (x+3,y+22), (x+18,y+22))
    pygame.draw.line   (surf,(200,200,200),
                             (x+18,y+22), (x+15,y+20))
    pygame.draw.line   (surf,(200,200,200),
                             (x+10,y+10), (x-5, y+25))
    pygame.draw.line   (surf,(200,200,200),
                             (x+10,y+10), (x+25, y+25))
```

The lander will be drawn at a location on the display window indicated by a pair of global variables **x** and **y**. The speed at which the lander is moving will be stored in variables **dx** and **dy**, which will be controlled by the keyboard presses of the user. The new position of the lander after each new frame is drawn will be (**x+dx, y+dy**).

Movement

The default motion for the craft is downwards due to gravity. During each iteration of the main loop, the craft moves in the increasing y direction, and because it is accelerating the value of the velocity changes too. If y is the current y coordinate and dy is the velocity then:

```
y = y + dy
dy = dy + 0.5
```

When the UP key is pressed, the craft should accelerate upwards, and it should continue to accelerate until the key is released. This means adding a value to **dy** to slow its descent or even make it move upwards.

So long as the UP key is depressed, which is to say a KEYUP has not yet been received, the upwards velocity (increase in **dy**) will continue to increase. When the UP key is depressed a flag is set to true, and when it is released the flag is set to False, and so long as the flag is true we perform **dy = dy − 0.3** each iteration. The flag is named **power**.

Movement to the left and right are done the same way; flags moveleft and moveright indicate the LEFT and RIGHT keys are depressed and motion in that direction should increase; this means changing the value of **dx**, the velocity in the x direction. Here is the event loop:

```
for event in pygame.event.get():
    if event.type == pygame.KEYDOWN:
        if event.key == pygame.K_UP:
            power = True
            sound.play()
        if event.key == pygame.K_LEFT:
            moveleft = True
        if event.key == pygame.K_RIGHT:
            moveright = True

    if event.type == pygame.KEYUP:
        if event.key == pygame.K_UP:
            power = False
            sound.stop()
        if event.key == pygame.K_LEFT:
            moveleft = False
        if event.key == pygame.K_RIGHT:
            moveright = False
```

When an engine is turned on fuel is consumed. As long as the UP key is pressed we consume 1 unit of fuel per iteration; sidewise motion uses 0.3 units, but only when the key is pressed. Motion continues regardless because of Newton's law but needs no fuel. Moving the lander happens after the event loop, and the code looks like this:

```
if moveleft:
    dx = dx - 1
    fuel = fuel - 0.3
elif moveright:
    dx = dx + 1
    fuel = fuel - 0.3
if power:
    fuel = fuel - 1
    dy = dy - 0.3
else:
    dy = dy + 0.5
x = int(x + dx)
y = int(y + dy)
```

FIGURE 7.20 The background (lunar landscape).

The Background

The lander is drawn over the top of a simple graphic that represents the lunar surface. The lander has landed when it touches the light brown region at the bottom of the image. It is displayed each time through the main loop, and is wider than the drawing window. It is possible to display different portions of it, allowing more levels.

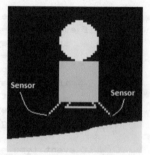

FIGURE 7.21 The pixels at the ends of the lander legs "sense" the color of the ground.

The lander has a special location at the bottom of each of the legs that is used to sense the landing. When the pixel in the drawing area is neither white nor black, then the sensor has touched the ground and the craft has landed.

If the landing has been detected, the game is won if the velocity **dy** at that time is 3 or less; otherwise, the lander has crashed. A function named landed evaluates whether the craft is down or not.

At this point the rest of the main loop can be provided: we must redraw the background, draw the lander in its proper location, and test to see if it has landed or not.

```
surf.blit (im, (-100,0))      # Draw background
draw_lander (x,y)             # Draw the lander
if fuel < 0:                  # If out of fuel, you lose.
    surf.fill ((255,0,0))
    lose = True
text("Fuel:"+str(int(fuel)), 10, 10) # Display fuel

if landed(x, y):              # If landed, how fast?
    if dy < 3:                # Slow, good news
        win = True
    else:                     # Too fast. Crash.
        lose = True
```

```
# Display the altitude and speed.
text ("Speed: "+str( int(dy*100)//100)+
           " height "+str(y), 200, 20)
pygame.display.update()
```

A few other things are done here. The fuel is checked, and if we're out of fuel the game is over. The flags **win** and **lose** indicate that the game is over and the player won or lost, respectively.

The current amount of fuel, altitude, and speed are displayed on the screen using a function named **text**. It is interesting to examine this function:

```
def text (s, x, y):
    global font
    text = font.render(s, 1, (200,200,0))
    pygame.draw.rect (surf, (0,0,0), (x, y,200, 20))
    surf.blit (text, (x,y))
```

Here the parameters x and y indicate the location of the text on the screen. The text is rendered into a local Surface and is blitted into the display surface. It is a convenient function to have.

Sound

There is only one sound, that being the engine. When the UP key is pressed, the engine is engaged and makes a noise. The sound is in a file "engine.wav" which is loaded at the beginning of the game. The event loop listed above shows that when the UP key is depressed, there is a call to **sound.play**(), and when the key is released, there is a call to **sound. stop**(). It's basically that simple.

Landing

Detecting a landing has a small set of possibilities. The function **landed** must return either **True** or **False**, and all situations have to be enumerated. Here is the function, annotated:

```def landed (x, y):``` ```global im, surf```	Parameters x and y define the origin of the lander graphic.
```if y>311:``` ```return True```	The lander has passed the bottom of the screen.
```if y<10:``` ```return False```	Lander is above the top of the screen.
```if x<6 or x>374:``` ```return False```	Lander is off the screen left or right.

(continued)

`    c1 = surf.get_at ((x+25,`
`y+26))`
`    if c1[0] != 0 and c1[0]`
`!= 255:`
`        return True`
	If the color of the pixel at the right lander leg is not black or white, then the lander is touching the ground.

`    c2 = surf.get_at ((x-5,`
`y+26))`
`    if c2[0] != 0 and c2[0]`
`!= 255:`
`        return True`
	If the color of the pixel at the left lander leg is not black or white, then the lander is touching the ground.

`return False`	Default return value is false.

Improvements

Two important additions could be made to this game. First, when the engine is on, there should be some kind of exhaust visible at the bottom of the lander. This is a perfect situation for a small animation.

Similarly, perhaps if the lander crashes, it should be seen to explode.

Other sounds are possible: the left and right engines possibly, the sound of a successful landing or a crash, and perhaps even some music.

Finally, a start screen showing the rules and controls is always a good idea in a computer game.

Conclusion

Pygame has a lot of features that have not been discussed in this brief chapter, but these can be found in books and in online documentation and tutorial pages. Here is a list of places to begin looking for more information:

http://www.pygame.org/docs/
Online documentation.

http://www.pygame.org/docs/tut/intro/intro.html
Tutorial.

http://www.cogsci.rpi.edu/~destem/gamedev/pygame.pdf
Cheat sheet.

8

HANDLING DATA

his chapter will be an examination of how certain kinds of data are represented and the consequences insofar as how computer programs can use these data. Python in particular will be used for this examination, although some of the discussion is more general. Of course, the discussion will be driven by practical things and by how things can be accomplished using Python.

Most data consists of measurements of something, and as such are fundamentally numeric. Astronomers measure the brightness of stars, as an example, and note how they vary or not as a function of time. The data consists of a collection of numbers that represent brightness on some arbitrary scale; the units of measurements are always in some sense arbitrary. However, units can be converted from one kind to another quite simply, so this is not a problem. Biologists frequently count things, so again their data is fundamentally numeric. Social scientists ask questions and collect answers into groups, again a numeric result.

Then there are search engines, which can be thought of as an extension of human memory and reasoning. The ability of humans to access information has improved hugely over the past twenty years. If the phrase "python data manipulation" is entered to the Google search engine, over half a million results are returned. True, many may not directly relate to the query as it was intended, but part of the problem will be in the phrasing of the request.

How is all of this done? It does take some clever algorithms and good programming, but it also requires a language that offers the right facilities.

Dictionaries

A Python *dictionary* is an important structure for dealing with data, and is the only important language feature that has not been discussed until now. One reason is that a dictionary is more properly an advanced structure that is implemented in terms of more basic ones. A *list*, for example, is a collection of things (integers, reals, strings) that is accessed by using an index, where the index is an integer. If the integer is given, the contents of the list at that location can be retrieved or modified.

A dictionary allows a more complex, expensive, and useful indexing scheme: it is accessed by content. Well, by a *description* of content at least. A dictionary can be indexed by a string, which in general would be referred to as a *key*, and the information at that location in the dictionary is said to be *associated* with that key. An example: a dictionary that returns the value of a color given the name. A color, as described in Chapter 7, is specified by a red, green, and blue component. A tuple such as (100,200,100) can be used to represent a color. So in a dictionary named **colors** the value of **colors['red']** might be (255,0,0) and **colors['blue']** is (0,0,255). Naturally, it is important to know what names are possible or the index used will not be legal and will cause an error. So **colors['copper']** may result in an index error, which for a dictionary is called a *KeyError*.

The Python syntax for setting up a dictionary differs from anything that has been seen before. The dictionary **colors** could be created in this way:

```
colors = {'red':(255, 0, 0), 'blue':(0,0,255),
'green':(0,255,0)}
```

The braces { . . . } enclose all of the things being defined as part of the dictionary. Each entry is a pair, with a key followed by a ":" followed by a data element. The pair 'red':(255,0,0) means that the key 'red' will be associated with the value (255,0,0) in this dictionary.

Now the name **colors** looks like a list, but it is indexed by a string:

```
print (colors['blue'])
```

The index is called a *key* when referring to a dictionary. That's because it is not really an index, in that the string can't directly address a location. Instead the key is searched for, and if it is a legal key (i.e., has been defined), the corresponding data element is selected. The definition of **colors** creates a list of keys and a list of data:

Location	Keys	Data
0	'red'	(255, 0, 0)
1	'blue'	(0, 0, 255)
2	'green'	(0, 255, 0)

When the expression **colors['blue']** is seen, the key 'blue' is searched for in the list of all keys. It is found at location 1, so the result of the expression is the data element at 1, which is (0,0,255). Python does all of this work each time a dictionary is accessed, so while it looks simple, it really involves quite a bit of work.

New associations can be made in assignment statements:

```
colors['khaki'] = (240,230,140)
```

Indeed, a dictionary can be created with an empty pair of braces and then have values given using assignments:

```
colors = {}
colors['red'] = (255, 0, 0)
     .   .   .
```

As with other variables, the value of an element in a dictionary can be changed. This would change the association with the key; there can only be one thing associated with a key. The assignment:

```
colors['red'] = (200.,0,0)
```

reassigns the value associated with the key 'red.' To delete it altogether use the **del()** function:

```
del(colors['blue'])
```

Other types can be used as keys in a dictionary. In fact, any immutable type can be used. Hence it is possible to create a dictionary that reverses the association of name to its RGB color, allowing the color to be used as the key and the name to be retrieved. For example:

```
names = {}
names[(255,0,0)] = 'red'
names[(0,255,0)] = 'green'
```

This dictionary uses tuples as keys. Lists can't be used because they are not immutable.

Functions for Dictionaries

The power of the store-fetch scheme in the dictionary is impressive. There are some methods that apply mainly to dictionaries and that can be useful in more complex programs. The method **keys()** returns the collection of all of the keys that can be used with a dictionary. So:

```
list(dict.keys())
```

is a list of all of the keys, and this can be searched before doing any complex operations on the dictionary. The list of keys is not in any specific order and if they need to be sorted, then:

```
sorted(dict.keys())
```

will do the job. The **del()** method has been used to remove specific keys, but **dict.clear()** will remove all of them.

The method **setdefault()** can establish a default value for a key that has not been defined. When an attempt is made to access a dictionary using a key, an error occurs if the key has not been defined for that dictionary. This method makes the key known so that no error will occur and give a value that can be returned for it; **None**, perhaps.

```
dict.setdefault(key, default=None)
```

Other useful functions include:

dict.copy() – returns a (shallow) copy of dictionary.

dict.fromkeys() –create a new dictionary setting keys and values.

For example, dict.fromkeys(("one", "two"), 3) creates {("one", 3), ("two", 3)}

dict.items() –returns a list of *dict*'s (key, value) tuple pairs.

dict.values() –returns list of dictionary *dict*'s values.

dict.update(dict2) –adds the key-value pairs from dictionary dict2 to dict.

The expression **key in dict** is True if the key specified exists in the dictionary dict.

Dictionaries and Loops

Dictionaries are intended for random access, but on occasion it is necessary to scan through parts or all of one. The trick is to create a list from the pairs in the dictionary and then loop through the list. For example:

```
for (key,value) in dict.items():
    print (key, " has the value ", value)
```

The keys are given in an internal order which is not alphabetical. Yet it is a simple matter to sort them:

```
for (key,value) in sorted(dict.items()):
    print (key, " has the value ", value)
```

By converting the dictionary pairs in a list, any of the operations on lists can be applied to a dictionary as well. It is even possible to use comprehensions to initialize a dictionary. For example:

```
d = {angle:sin(radians(angle)) for angle in (0,45.,90., 135.,
180.)}
```

creates a dictionary of the sines of some angles indexed by the angle.

Arrays

For programmers who have used other languages, Python *lists* have many of the properties of an *array*, which in C++ or Java is a collection of consecutive memory locations that contain the same type of value. *Lists* may be designed to make operations such as concatenation efficient, which means that a *list* may not be the most efficient way to store things. A Python *array* is a class that mimics the array type of other languages and offers efficiency in storage, exchanging that for flexibility.

Only certain types can be stored in an array, and the type of the array is specified when it is created. For example:

```
data = array('f', [12.8, 5.4, 8.0, 8.0, 9.21, 3.14])
```

creates an array of 6 floating point numbers; the type is indicated by the 'f' as the first parameter to the constructor. This concept is unlike the Python norm of types being dynamic and malleable. An *array* is an array of one kind of thing, and an *array* can only hold a restricted set of types.

The type code, the first parameter to the constructor, can have one of 13 values, but the most commonly used ones will be:

'b' A C++ char type
'B' A C++ unsigned char type
'i': A C++ int type
'l': A C++ long type
'f': A C++ float type
'd': A C++ double type

Arrays are class objects and are provided in the built-in module *array*, which must be imported:

```
from array import array
```

An *array* is a sequence type, and has the basic properties and operations that Python provides all sequence types. Array elements can be assigned to and can be used in expressions, and arrays can be searched and extended like other sequences. There are some features of arrays that are unique:

frombytes (s)	The string argument **s** is converted into byte sequences and appended to the array.
fromfile(f, num)	Reads **num** items from the file object **f** and appends them. An integer, for example, is one item.
fromlist (x)	Appends the elements from the list x to the array.
tobytes()	Converts the array into a sequence of bytes in machine representation.
tofile(f)	Writes the array as a sequence of bytes to the file **f**.

In most cases arrays are used to speed up numerical operations, but they can also be used (and will be in the next section) to access the underlying representations of numbers.

Formatted Text, Formatted I/O

There is a generally believed theory among many users of data, including some engineers and financial analysts, that if numbers line up in nice columns then they must be correct. This is obviously not true, but appearances can matter a great deal, and numbers that do *not* line up properly for easy reading look sloppy and give people the impression that they may not be as carefully prepared as they should have been. The Python **print()** function as used so far simply prints a collection of variables and constants with no real attention to a format. Each one is printed in the order specified with a space between them. Sometimes that's good enough.

The Python versions since 2.7 have incorporated a string **format()** method that allows a programmer to specify how values should be placed within a string. The idea is to create a string that contains the formatted output and then print the string. A simple example is:

```
s = "x={} y={}"
fs = s.format (121.2, 6)
```

The string **fs** now contains "x=121.2 y=6." The braces within the format string **s** hold the place for a value. The **format**() method lists values to be placed into the string, and with no other information given it does so in order of appearance, in this case 121.2 followed by 6. The first pair of braces is replaced by the first value, 121.2, and the second pair of braces is replaced by the second value, which is 6. Now the string **fs** can be printed.

This is not how it is usually done, though. Because this is usually part of the output process, it is often placed within the **print**() call:

```
print ("x={} y={}".format(121.2, 6) )
```

where the **format**() method is referenced from the string constant. No actual formatting is done by this particular call, it is merely a conversion to string and a substitution of values. The way formatting is done depends on the type of the value being formatted, the most common types being strings, integers, and floats. An example will be illuminating.

Example: NASA Meteorite Landing Data

NASA publishes a huge amount of data on its web sites, and one of these is a collection of meteorite landings. It covers many years and has over 4800 entries. The task assigned here is to print a nicely formatted report on selected parts of the data. The data on the file has its fields separated by commas, and there are ten of them: name, id, nametype, recclass, mass, Fall, year, reclat, reclong, and GeoLocation. The report requires that the name, recclass, mass, reclat, and reclong be arranged in a nicely formatted set of columns.

Reading the data is a matter of opening the file, which is named "met. txt," and calling **readline**(), then creating a list of the fields using **split**(","). If this is done and the fields are simply printed using **print**(), the result is messy. An abbreviated example is (simulated data):

```
infile = open ("met.txt", "r")
inline = infile.readline()

while inline !="":
    inlist = inline.split(",")
    mass = float(inlist[4])
    lat =  float(inlist[7])
    long = float(inlist[8])
    print (inlist[0], inlist[3], inlist[4], inlist[7],
            inlist[8])
    inline = infile.readline()
infile.close()
```

The result is, as predicted, messy:

```
Ashdon H5 121.13519985254874 89.85924301385958
-126.27404435776049
Arbol Solo H6 66.94777134343516 25.567048824444797
160.58088365396014
Baldwyn L6 47.6388587105465 -7.708508536783924
-81.22266156597777
Ankober L6 15.265523451122064 -32.01862330869428
102.31244557598723
Ankober LL6 57.584802700693885 -84.85880091616322
106.31130649523368
Ash Creek L6 62.130089525516155 76.02832670618457
-140.03422105516938
Almahata Sitta LL5 30.476879105555653 -12.906745404586
47.411816322674
```

Nothing lines up in columns, and the numbers show an impossible degree of precision. Also, there should be headings.

The first field to be printed is called *name*, and it is a string; it is the name of the location where the observation was made. The print statement simply adds a space after printing it, and so the next thing prints immediately following. Things do not line up. Formatting a string for output involves specifying how much space to allow and whether the string should be centered or aligned to the left or right side of the area where it will be printed. Applying a left alignment to the string variable named **place-name** in a field of 16 characters would be done as follows:

'{:16s}'.format(placename)

The braces, which have previously been empty, contain formatting directives. Empty braces mean *no formatting*, and simply hold the place for a value. A full format could contain a name, a conversion part, and a specification:

{ [name]   ['!' conversion]   [':' specification] }

where optional parts are in square brackets. Thus, the minimal format specification is '{}'. In the example "{:16s}" there is no name and no conversion parts, only a specification. After the ':' is '16s,' meaning that the data to be placed here is a string, and that 16 characters should be allowed for it. It will be left aligned by default, so if **placename** was "Atlanta," the result of the formatting would be the string "Atlanta   ", left aligned in a 16-character string. Unfortunately, if the original string is longer than 16 characters, it will not be truncated, and all of the characters will be placed in the resulting string even if it makes it too long.

To right align a string, simply place a ">" character immediately following the ":". So:

"{:>16s}".format("Atlanta")

would be "   Atlanta." Placing a "<" character there does a left alignment (the default) and "^" means to center it in the available space. The alignment specifications apply to numbers as well as strings.

The first two values to be printed in the example are the city name, which is in **inlist[0]**, and the meteorite class, which is **inlist[3]**. Formatting these is done as follows:

```
s = '{:16s} {:10s}'.format(inlist[0], inlist[3])
```

Both Strings Will Be Left Aligned

Numeric formats are more complicated. For integers there is the total space to allow, and also how to align it and what to do with the sign and leading zeros. The formatting letter for an integer is "d," so the following are legal directives and their meaning:

Format	Explanation	result for value 1234
'{:5d}'	An integer in a 5 character space, right aligned	" 1234"
'{:>5d}'	An integer in a 5 character space, right aligned	" 1234"
'{:<7d}'	An integer in a 7 character space, left aligned	"1234 "
'{:07d}'	An integer right aligned in a 7 character space filled on the left with zeros.	"0001234"
'{:,7d}'	A right aligned integer in 7 character space with a ',' every 3 digits	" 1,234"
'{:7x}'	A right aligned integer in hexadecimal.	" 4D2"

Floating point numbers have the extra issue of the decimal place. The format character is often "f," but can be "e" for exponential format or "g" for general format, meaning the system decides whether to use "f" or "e."

Otherwise, the formatting of floating point is like that of previous versions of Python and like that of C and C++:

Format for Value 12.321	Explanation	Result
'{:.3f}'	3 digits right of the decimal	'12.321'
'{:6.2f}'	6 digits, 3 to the right of the decimal	' 12.32'
'{:>8.1}'	5 digits, 1 to the right, left adjusted	' 12.3'
'{:8e}'	8 places, exponential form	'1.232100e+01'
'{:8g}'	8 places, system decides	' 12.321'

The next three values to be printed are floating point: the mass of the meteorite and the location, as latitude and longitude. Printing each of these as 7 places, 2 to the right of the decimal, would seem to work. Or, as a format: '{:7.2f}'.

The solution to the problem is now at hand. The data is read line by line, converted into a list, and then the fields are formatted and printed in two steps:

```
infile = open ("met.txt", "r")
inline = infile.readline()
print ("      Place      Class          Mass   Latitude
Longitude")
while inline !="":
    inlist = inline.split(",")
    mass = float(inlist[4])
    lat = float(inlist[7])
    long = float(inlist[8])
    print('{:16s} {:14s} {:7.2f}'.format(inlist[0],inlist[3],
        mass),end="")
    print ('  {:7.2f}      {:7.2f}'.format(lat, long))
    inline = infile.readline()
infile.close()
```

The result is:

Place	Class	Mass	Latitude	Longitude
Bloomington	L5	13.58	9.53	-150.85
Bogou	L6	121.09	-66.28	-53.08
Alessandria	L4	106.11	63.68	10.96
Bo Xian	L5	85.92	0.33	-50.28
Ashdon Eucrite-mmict	6.59	-88.22	-178.84	
Berduc	L6	111.76	-64.20	107.10

...

There are many more formatting directives, and a huge number of their combinations. Future examples may expose them.

Advanced Data Files

File operations were discussed Chapter 5, but the discussion was limited to files containing text. Text is crucial because it is how humans communicate with the computer; people are unhappy about having to enter binary numbers. On the other hand, text files take up more space than needed to hold the information they do. Each character requires at least one byte. The number 3.1415926535 thus takes up 12 bytes, but if stored as a floating-point number, it needs only 4 or 8 depending on precision.

The file system on most computers also permits a variety of operations that have not been discussed. This includes reading from any point in a file, appending data to files, and modifying data. The need for processing data effectively is a main reason for computers to exist at all, so it is important to know as much as possible about how to program a computer for these purposes.

Binary Files

A *binary* file is one that does not contain text, but instead holds the raw, internal representation of its data. Of course, all files on a computer disk are binary in the strict sense, because they all contain numbers in binary form, but a binary file in this discussion does not contain information that can be read by a human. Binary files can be more efficient than other kinds, both in file size (smaller) and the time it takes to read and write them (less). Many standard files types, such as MP3, exist as binary files, so it is important to understand how to manipulate them.

Example: Create a File of Integers

The *array* type holds data in a form that is more natural for most computers than does a list, and also has the **tofile**() method built in. If a collection of integers is to be written as a binary file, a first step is to place them into an array. If a set of 10000 consecutive integers are to be written to a file named "ints" the first step is to import the array class and open the output file. Notice that the file is open in "wb" mode, which means "write binary":

```
from array import array
output_file = open('ints', 'wb')
```

Now create an array to hold the elements and fill the array with the consecutive integers:

```
arr = array('i')
for k in range (10000, 20000):
    arr.append(k)
```

Finally, write the data in the array to the file:

```
arr.tofile(out)
out.close()
```

This file has a size listed as 40kb on a Windows PC. A file having the same integers written as text is 49kb. This is not exactly a huge space saving, but it does add up.

Reading these values back is just as simple:

```
inf = open ('ints', 'rb')
arrin = array('i')
for k in range (0, 10001):
    try:
        arrin.fromfile(inf, 1)
    except:
        break
    print (arrin[k])
inf.close()
```

The **try** is used to catch an end-of-file error in cases where the number of items on the file is not known in advance. Or just because always doing so is a good idea.

Sometimes a binary file will contain data that is all of the same type, but that situation is not very common. It is more likely that the file will have strings, integers, and floats intermixed. Imagine a file of data for bank accounts or magazine subscriptions; the information included would be names and addresses, dates, financial values, and optional data depending on the specific situation. Some customers have multiple accounts, for example. How can binary files be created that contain more than one kind of information? By using *structs*.

The Struct Module

The *struct* module permits variables and objects of various types to be converted into what amounts to a sequence of bytes. It is a common claim that this is in order to convert between Python forms and C forms, because C has a *struct* type (short for *structure*). However, many files exist that consist of mixed type data in raw (i.e., machine compatible) form that have been created by many programs in many languages. It is possible that C is singled out because the name *struct* was used.

Example: A Video Game High Score File

Video game players need little incentive to try hard to win a game, but for many years a special reward is given to the better players. The game "remembers" the best players and lists them at the beginning and end of the game. This kind of ego boost is a part of the reward system of the game. The game program stores the information on a file in descending order of score. The data that is saved is usually the player's name or initials, the score, and the date. This mixes string with numeric data.

Consider that the player's name is held in a variable **name**, the score is an integer **score**, and the date is a set of three strings **year**, **month**, and **day**. In this situation the size of each value needs to be fixed, so allow 32 characters for the name, 4 for year, 2 for month, and 2 for day. The file was created with the name first, then the score, then the year, month, and day. The order matters because it will be read in the same order that it was written. On the file the data will look like this:

```
cccccccccccccccccccccccccccccccc iiii   cccc    cc      cc
Player's name                    Score   Year   Month    Day
```

Each letter in the first string represents a byte in the data for this entry. The "c"s represent characters; the "i"s represent bytes that are part of an integer. There are 44 bytes in all, which is the size of one data *record*, which is what one set of related data is generally called. A file contains the records for all of the elements in the data set, and in this case a record is the data for one player, or at least one time that the player played the game. There can be multiple entries for a player.

One way to convert mixed data like this into a *struct* is to use the **pack()** method. It takes a format parameter first, which indicates what the *struct* will consist of in terms of bytes. Then the values are passed that will be converted into components of the final struct. For the example here the call to **pack()** would be:

```
s = pack ("32si4s2s2s", name, score, year, month, day)
```

The format string is "32si4s2s2s"; there are 5 parts to this, one for each of the values to be packed:

32s is a 32-character-long string. It should be of type *bytes*.
i   is one integer. However, **2i** would be two integers, and **12i** is 12 integers.
4s is a 4-character-long string.
2s is a 2-character-long string.

Other important format items are:

c is a character
f is a float
d is a double-precision float

The value returned from **pack()** has type *bytes*, and in this case is 44 bytes long. The high score file consists of many of these records, all of which are the same size. A record can be written to a file using **write()**. So, a program that writes just one such record would be:

```
from struct import *

f = open ("hiscores", "wb")
name = bytes("Jim Parker", 'UTF-8')
score = 109800
year = b"2015"
month = b"12"
day = b"26"
s = pack ("32si4s2s2s", name, score, year, month, day)
f.write(s)
```

Reading this file involves first reading the string of bytes that represented a data record. Then it is *unpacked*, which is the reverse of what **pack()** does, and the variables passed to the **unpack()** function to be filled with data. The **unpack()** method takes a format string as the first parameter, the same kind of format string as **pack()** uses. It will return a tuple. An example that reads the record in the above code would be:

```
from struct import *

f = open("hiscores", "rb")
s = f.read(44)
name,score,year,month,day = unpack("32si4s2s2s", s)
name = name.decode("UTF-8")
year = year.decode("UTF-8")
month = month.decode("UTF-8")
day = day.decode("UTF-8")
```

The data returned by unpack are *bytes*, and need to be converted into strings before being used in most cases. Note the input mode on the **open**() call is "rb," read binary.

A file in this format has been provided, and is named simply 'hiscore'. When a player plays the game, they will enter their name; the computer knows their score and the date. A new entry must be made in the 'hiscore' file with this new score in it. How is that done?

Start with the new player data for *Karl Holter*, with a score of 100000. To update the file it is opened and records are read and written to a new temporary file (named 'tmp') until one is found that has a smaller score than the 100000 that Karl achieved. Then Karl's record is written to the temporary file, and the remainder of 'hiscores' is copied there. This creates a new file named 'tmp' that has Karl's data added to it, and in the correct place. Now that file can be copied to 'hiscores' replacing the old file, or the file named 'tmp' can be renamed as 'hiscores'. This is called a *sequential file update*.

Renaming the file requires access to some of the operating system functions in the module *os*; in particular:

```
os.rename ("tmp", "hiscores")
```

Random Access

It seems natural to begin reading a file from the beginning, but that is not always necessary. If the data that is desired is located at a known place in the file, then the location being read from can be set to that point. This is a natural consequence of the fact that disk devices can be positioned at any location at any time. Why not files too?

The function that positions the file at a specific byte location is **seek**():

```
f.seek(44)      # Position the file at byte 44,
                # which is the second record in the hiscores file.
```

It's also possible to position the file relative to the current location:

```
f.seek(44, 1)   # Position the file 44 bytes from this location,
                # which skips over the next record in hiscores.
```

A file can be rewound so that it can be read over again by calling **f.seek(0)**, positioning the file at the beginning. It is otherwise difficult to make use of this feature unless the records on the file are of a fixed size, as they are in the file 'hiscores', or the information on record sizes is saved in the file. Some files are intended from the outset to be used as random access files. Those files have an index that allows specific records to be read on demand. This is very much like a *dictionary*, but on a file. Assuming that the score for player *Arlen Franks* is needed, the name is searched for in the index. The result is the byte offset for Arlen's high score entry in the file.

Arlen's record starts at byte 352 (8th record * 44 bytes). He just played the game again and improved his score. Why not update his record on the file? The file needs to be open for input *and* output, so mode "rb+", meaning open a binary file for input and output, would work in this case. Then position the file to Arlen's record, create a new record, and write that one record. This is new—being able to both read and write the same file seems odd, but if the data being written is exactly the same size as the record on the file, then no harm should come from it. The program is:

```
# read and print hiscore file
from struct import *

f = open ("hiscores", "r+b")   # Open binary file, input and output
pos = 44*8              # Desired record is 8, 44 bytes per
f.seek(pos)             # Seek to that position one the file
s = f.read(44)          # Read the target record
name = b'Arlen Franks'          # Make a new one with a new score
score = 100300
year = b'201 5'
month = b'12'
day = b'26'             # Pack the new data
ss = pack("32si4s2s2s", name, score, year, month, day)
f.seek (44*8)           # Seek the original position again!
f.write(ss)             # Write the new data over the old
f.close ()              # Close the file
```

This works fine, provided that the position of Arlen's data in the file is known. It does not maintain the file in descending order, though.

Example: Maintaining the High Score File in Order

The circumstances of the new problem are that a player only appears in the high score file once and the file is maintained in descending order of score. If a player improves their score, then their entry should move closer to the beginning of the file. This is a more difficult problem than before, but one that is still practical. So, presume that a player has achieved a new score. The entire process should be:

Get the player's old score.	Read the file, get the player's record, unpack it.
Is the new score larger?	If not, close the file. Done.
Yes, so find out where the score belongs, in the file.	Look at successively preceding records until one is found that has a larger score.
Place the new record where it belongs.	Copy the records from the new position for the record ahead one position until the old position is reached.

The process is like moving a playing card closer to the top of the deck while leaving the other cards in the same order. It's probably more efficient to move the record while searching for the correct position, though. Each time the previous record is examined, if it does not have a larger score, then the record being placed is copied ahead one position. This results in a pretty compact program, given the nature of the problem, but it is a bit tricky to get right. For example, what if the new score is the highest? What if the current high score gets a higher score?

## CHAPTER 9

COMMUNICATION USING PYTHON

In the age of high speed Internet, social media, podcasts, blogs, and wikis, input from the keyboard and output to the screen is not enough. The wide world outside of the desktop beckons, and a programmer with a knowledge of Python and the relevant modules can respond.

Can a computer communicate with another one? Of course. Can a program send Email? Yes, that's what a mail program like *Thunderbird* or *Outlook* does. Can a program be written that reads tweets as they are sent? Sure, but there is a price. That is: these things are done according to someone else's rules. The first Email was sent in 1971 on a private network named *Arpanet*. It sent mail between distinct computers, rather than sending messages between users on a specific machine. In 1972 Unix Email was made available, and was networked in 1978; that was the start of something big.

The sender and receiver had to agree on how to encode and decode a message, and how to access it from the network. To send mail between different computers always requires a standard, a scheme that is agreed upon by implementers of the system. Otherwise, mail can only be sent between UNIX systems, or Windows, or iOS. Email, to be practical, needs to be more flexible. It needs to be ubiquitous, and so all need to agree on a standard for how Email can be sent and received. A standard was eventually agreed on, and it was called the *Simple Mail Transfer Protocol* (SMTP) and was established in 1982.

This was seven years before the World Wide Web, so Email really represents the first practical way to communicate between computers over a long distance. FTP happened at about the same time. The enabling technology for the Web, TCP/IP, came next. All of these developments in networking and software combined to create the modern interconnected society, but all are based on a collection of rules that software must agree to (*protocols*) if they are to make use of the network infrastructure. This is an example of *design by contract*, in which designers create formal specifications for components, and using those involves a kind-of contract or agreement between programmers developing client software and those who built the modules and designed the protocols.

There are high-level programs that provide a good user interface to the Internet and that implement these protocols beneath their visual presentation. When using Python a collection of modules are used that handle the very low-level details, but the interface to the programmer exposes the protocol. Some of these modules are provided in a standard Python installation (*smtplib*, *email*), and some are not (*MPI*, *Tweepy*) and will have to be installed before the code in this chapter will run.

When communicating with another machine, a key issue is that of *authentication*. Almost all protocols require that a connection be formed between the two computers, using some kind of identification of those machines such as their IP address. Then the one initializing the connection must prove that it has permission to do what it is about to do. This resembles logging in, and involves a user identification and a password of some type. Once the user has been identified, there is an exchange of messages that tell the remote computer what is desired of it, and that allow information to be returned to the caller. This process is nearly universal, but it takes somewhat different forms on different systems.

Email

Email is a good example of a *client-server* system, and one that gets used millions of times each minute. The Email program on a PC is the client, and allows a user to enter text messages, specify destinations, attach images, and all of the features expected by such a program. This client packages the Email message (data) according to the *Simple Message Transfer Protocol* (SMTP) and sends that to another computer on the Internet, the Email server. An Email user must have an account on the server for this to work so they can be identified and the user can receive replies; so, the process is: log into the Email server, then send the SMTP message to the Email server program on that server. Thus the client side of the contract is to create a properly formatted message, to log into the server properly, and pass the message to it.

Now the server does the work. Given the destination of the message, it searches for the server that is connected to that destination. For example, given the address **xyz@gmail.com**, the server for gmail.com is located. Then the Email message is sent across the network to that server. The server software at that end reads the message and places it into the mailbox, which is really just a directory on a disk drive connected to the server, for the specified use **xyz**. The mail message is essentially a text file at this point.

This description is simplified but essentially accurate, and describes what has to be done by a program that is supposed to send an Email message. The Python module that permits the sending of Email implements the protocol and offers the programmer ways to specify the parameters, like the destination and the message. The interface is implemented as a set of functions. The library needed for this is *smtplib*, a part of the standard Python system.

Example: Send an Email

Sending an Email message starts with establishing a connection between the client computer and the user's mail server, the one on which they have an account (user name and password). For the purposes here a Gmail (Google) server will be used, which complicates the issue a tiny bit. The Email accounts in the example are also Gmail ones, and these can be had for free from Google.

The program must declare *smtplib* as an imported module. The sending address and the receiving address will be the same in this example, but this is just a test. Normally this will not be the situation. The Email address is the user ID for Gmail authentication and the password is defined by the user. These are all just strings.

```
import smtplib

LOGIN = yourloginID       # Login User ID for Gmail, string
PASSWD = yourpassword     # Login password for Gmail, string
sndr = pythontextbook@gmail.com   # Sender's email address
rcvr = pythontextbook@gmail.com   # Receiver's email address
```

Part of the SMTP scheme is a syntax for Email messages. There is a header at the beginning that specifies the sender, receiver, and subject of the message. These are used to format the message, not to route it—the receiver address is specified later. A simple such message looks like this:

```
From: user_me@gmail.com
To: user_you@gmail.com
Subject: Just a message
```

A string must be constructed that contains this information:

```
msgt = "From: user_me@gmail.com\n"
msgt = msgt + "To: user_you@gmail.com\n"
msgt = msgt + "Subject: Just a message\n"
msgt = msgt + "\n"
```

Now the body of the message is attached to this string. This is the part of the Email that is important to the sender:

```
msgt = msgt + "Attention: This message was sent by Python!\n"
```

The string variable **msgt** now holds the whole message. This message is in the format defined by the Multipurpose Internet Mail Extensions (MIME) standard. The next step for the program is to try to establish a connection with the sender's Email server. For this the *smtp* module is needed, specifically the **SMTP()** function. It is called passing the name of the user's Email server as a parameter, and it returns a variable that references that server. In this example that variable is named server:

```
server = smtplib.SMTP('smtp.gmail.com')
```

If it is not possible to connect to the server for some reason, then an error will occur. It is therefore a good idea to place this in a try-except block:

```
try:
    server = smtplib.SMTP('smtp.gmail.com')
except:
    print ("Error occurred. Can't connect")
else:
```

Now comes the complexity that Gmail and some other servers introduce. What has happened after the call to **smtplib.SMTP()** is that a communications session has been opened up. There is now an active connection between the client computer and the server at *smtp.gmail.com*. Some servers demand a level of security that, among other things, ensures that other parties can't modify or even read the message. This is accomplished using a protocol named *Transport Layer Security* (TLS), the details of which are not completely relevant because the modules take care of it. However, to send data to *smtp.gmail.com*, the server must be told to begin using TLS:

```
server.starttls()
```

Now the user must be authenticated using their ID and password:

```
server.login(LOGIN,PASSWD)
```

Only now can a message be sent, and only if the login ID and password are correct. The sender is the string **sndr**, the recipient is **rcvr**, and the message is **msgt**:

```
server.sendmail(sndr, rcvr, msgt)
```

Now that the message has been sent, it is polite to close the session. Logging off of the server is done as follows:

```
server.quit()
```

This program will send one Email, but it can be easily modified to send many Emails one after the other. It can be modified to read the message from the keyboard, or perform any of the functions of a typical Email-sending program.

The module Email can be invoked to format the message in MIME form. The function **MIMEText(s)** converts the message string **s** into an internal form, which is a MIME message. Fields like the subject and sender can be added to the message, and then it is sent as was done before. For example:

```
import smtplib
from email.mime.text import MIMEText

LOGIN = yourloginID
PASSWD = yourpassword

fp = open ("message.txt", "r")     # Read the message from a file
mtest = fp.read()
# Or: simply use a string
#mtest = "A message from Python: Merry Christmas."
fp.close()
```

```
msg = MIMEText (mtest)              # Create a MIME string
sndr = pythontextbook@gmail.com     # Sender's Email
rcvr = pythontextbook@gmail.com     # Recipient's Email
msg['Subject'] = 'Mail from Python' # Add Subject to
                                      the message
msg['From'] = sndr                  # Add sender to the message
msg['To'] = rcvr                    # Add recipient to the message

# Send the message using Google's SMTP server, as before
s = smtplib.SMTP('smtp.gmail.com')  # localhost could work
s.starttls()
s.login (LOGIN, PASSWD)
s.send_message(msg)
s.quit()
```

Using **MIMEText()** to create the message avoids having to format it correctly using basic string operations.

Figure 9.1 outlines the procedure for sending an Email using Python.

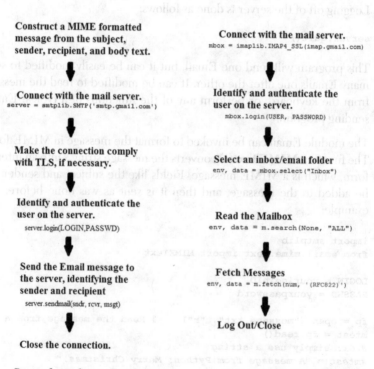

FIGURE 9.1 Reading and sending Email using Python.

Reading Email

Reading Email is more complicated than writing it. The content of an Email is often a surprise, and so a reader must be prepared to parse anything that might be sent. Which mailbox will be looked at, and when a user reads Email their mailbox often has more than one message in it; how can they be distinguished? In addition, the protocol for retrieving mail from a server is different from that used to send it; in fact there are two competing protocols: POP and IMAP.

The *Post Office Protocol* (POP) is the older of the two schemes, although it has been updated a few times. It certainly allows the basic requirements of a mail reader, which is to download and delete a message in a remote mailbox (i.e., on the server). The *Internet Message Access Protocol* (IMAP) is intended for use by many Email clients, and so messages tend not to be deleted until that is requested. When setting up an Email client, one of these protocols usually has to be specified, and then it will be used from then on. The example here will use IMAP.

Example: Display the Subject Headers for Emails in Inbox

An outline for the process of reading Email is sketched on the right-hand side of Figure 13.1. Reading Email uses a different module that was used to send Email: *imaplib*, for reading from an IMAP server. The function names are different from those in *smtplib*, but the purpose of some of them is the same. The first three steps in reading Email are:

```
import imaplib
server = 'imap.gmail.com'      # Gmail's IMAP server
USER = 'your email'            # User ID
PASSWORD = "password"          # Mask this password
EMAIL_FOLDER = "Inbox"

mbox = imaplib.IMAP4_SSL(server)  # Connect to the server
mbox.login(USER, PASSWORD)        # Authenticate (log in)
```

The next step is to select a mailbox to read. Each has a name, and is really just a directory someplace. The variable **mbox** is a class instance of a class named *imaplib.IMAP4_SSL*, the details of which can be found in many places including the Internet. It has a method named **select()** that allows the examination of a mailbox, given its name (a string). The string is a variable named EMAIL_FOLDER which contains "Inbox," and the call to select() that essentially opens the inbox is:

```
z = mbox.select(EMAIL_FOLDER)
```

The return value is a tuple. The first element indicates success or failure, and if z[0] contains the string "OK," and then the mailbox is open. The usual alternative is "NO." The second element of the tuple indicates how many messages there are, but it is in an odd format. If there are 2 messages, as in the example, this string is *b'2'*; if there were 3 messages it would be *b'3'*; and so on. These are called message sequence numbers.

Having opened the mailbox, the next step is to read it and extract the messages. The protocol requires that the mailbox be searched for the messages that are wanted. The *imaplib.IMAP4_SSL* class offers the **search()** method for this, the simplest form being:

```
mbox.search(None, "ALL")
```

which returns all of the messages in the mailbox. IMAP provides search functionality, and all this method does is connect to it, which is why it seems awkward to use. The first parameter specifies a character set, and None allows it to default to a general value. The second parameter specifies a search criterion as a string. There are dozens of parameters that can be used here and the documentation for IMAP should be examined in detail for solutions to specific problems. However, some of the more useful tags include:

ANSWERED: Messages that have been answered.

BCC <string>: Messages with a specific string in the BCC field.

BEFORE <date>: Messages whose date (not time) is earlier than the specified one.

HEADER <field-name> <string>: A specified field in the header contains the string.

SUBJECT <string>: Messages that contain the specified string in the SUBJECT field.

TO <string>: Messages that contain the specified string in the TO field.

UNSEEN: Messages that do not have the \Seen flag set.

So, a call to **search()** that looks for the text 'Python' in the subject line would be:

```
mbox.search(None, "SUBJECT Python")
```

The search() function returns a tuple again, where the first component is a status string (i.e., "OK," "NO," "BAD") and the second is a list of messages satisfying the search criteria in the same format as before. If the second message is the only match, this string will be **b'2'**. If the first three match it will be **b'1 2 3'**.

Finally, the messages are read, or *fetched*. The *imaplib.IMAP4_SSL* class has a **fetch**() method to do this, and it again takes some odd parameters. What a programmer thinks of the interface or the API or, in other words, the *contract*, is not important. What must be done is to satisfy the requirements and accept the data as it is offered. The **fetch**() method accepts two parameters: the first is the indication of which message is desired. The first message is *b'1'*, the second is *b'2'*, and so on. The second parameter is an indicator of what it is that should be returned. The header? If so, pass '(RFC822.HEADER)' as the parameter. Why? Because they ask for it. RFC822 is the name of a protocol. If the Email body is wanted then pass '(RFC822.TEXT)'. A short list of possibilities is:

RFC822	- Everything
RFC822.HEADER	- No body, header only
RFC822.TEXT	- Body only
RFC822.SIZE	- Message size
UID	- Message identifier

Multiple of these specifiers can be passed; for example:

```
mbox.fetch(num, '(UID RFC822.TEXT RFC822.HEADER)')
```

returns a tuple having three parts: the ID, the body, and the header. By the way, the header tends to be exceptionally long, 40 lines or so, and is mostly uninteresting to a specific application. For this example, the only part of the header that is interesting is the "Subject" part. Fields in the header are separated by the characters '\r\n' so they are easy to extract in a call to split(). Eliminating the header data for a moment, the call:

```
(env, data) = mbox.fetch(num, '(UID RFC822.TEXT)')
```

results in a tuple that has an "envelope" that should indicate "OK" (the **env** variable). The data part is a string that contains the UID and the text body of the message. For example:

```
[(b'2 (UID 22 RFC822.TEXT {718}', b"Got a collection of old
45's for sale. Contact me.\r\n\r\n-- \r\n"), b')']
```

This says that this is message 2 and shows the text of that message.

This example is supposed to print all of the subject headers in this mailbox. The call to **fetch**() should extract the header only:

```
(env, data) = mbox.fetch(num, '(RFC822.HEADER)')
```

The details of IMAP are complex enough that it is easy to forget what the original task was, which was to print the subject lines from the messages in the mailbox. All of the relevant methods have been described and completing the program is possible. The entire program is:

```
import imaplib

server = 'imap.gmail.com'              # IMAP Server
USER = "your email"                    # USER ID
PASSWORD = ""                          # Mask this password
EMAIL_FOLDER = "Inbox"                 # Which mailbox?
mbox = imaplib.IMAP4_SSL(server)       # Connect
mbox.login(USER, PASSWORD)             # Authenticate
env, data = mbox.select(EMAIL_FOLDER)  # Select the mailbox
if env == 'OK':                        # Did it work?
    print ("Printing subject headers: ", EMAIL_FOLDER)
    env, data = mbox.search(None, "ALL")
# Select the messages wanted.
    if env != 'OK':                    # Are there any?
        print ("No messages.", env)    # Nope.
        exit()
    for num in data[0].split():
# For each selected message b'1 2 3 ...'
        (env, data) = mbox.fetch(num, '(RFC822.HEADER)')
# Read it
        if env != 'OK':
            print ("ERROR getting message", num, ", ", env)
            break
        s = str(data[0][1])
# Look for the string "Subject" in the header
        k = s.find("Subject")
        if (k>=0):         # Found it?
            s = s[k:] # Extract the string to the next '\r'
        k = s.find('\\r')
        s = s[:k]
        print (s)                      # And print it.
    mbox.close()
else:
    print ("No such mailbox as ", EMAIL_FOLDER)
mbox.logout()
```

Typical output would be:

Printing subject headers: Inbox
Subject: Contents of Chapter 13
Subject: 45 RPM
Subject: another Email

The point of this section was to demonstrate how a Python program, or any program for that matter, must comply with external specifications when interfacing with sophisticated software systems, and to introduce the concept of a protocol, a contract between developers. Of course a program that can send Email is useful by itself.

Communication Between Processes

Underneath the FTP and Email protocols, which allow interfaces to applications, lies a communications layer, the programs that actually send bytes between computers or between programs on the same computer. It is conducted very much like a conversation. One person, the client, initiates the conversation ("Hi there!"). The other (the server) responds ("Hello. Nice to see you."). Now it is the client's turn again. They take turns *sending* and *accepting* messages until one says "goodbye." These messages might contain Email, or FTP data, or TV programs. This layer does not care what the data is; none of its business, really. Its job is to deliver it.

Data are delivered in *packets*, each containing a certain amount. In order for the client to deliver the data, there must be a server willing to connect to it. The client needs to know the address of a server, just as an FTP address or Email destination was required before, but now all that is needed is the host name and a *port number*. A port is really a logical construction, something akin to an element of a list. If two programs agree to share data by having one of them place it in location 50001 of a list and the other one read it from there, it gives an approximate idea of what a port is. Some port numbers are assigned and should not be used for anything else; FTP and Email have assigned ports. Others are available for use, and any two processes can agree to use one.

A module named socket, based on the interprocess communication scheme on UNIX of the same name, is used with Python to send messages back and forth. To create an example two computers should be used, one being the client and one the server, and the IP address of the server is required too.

Example: A Server That Calculates Squares

The client will open a communications link (socket) to the server, which has a known IP address. The server will engage in a short handshake (exchange of strings) and then expect to receive a number for the client. The client will send an integer, the server will receive it, square it, and send back the answer. This simple exchange is really the basis for all communications between computers: one machine sends information, the other receives it, processes it, and returns a reply based on the data it received.

The client: will begin the conversation. It creates a connection, a socket, to the server using the **socket**() function of the **socket** module. Protocols must be specified, and the most common ones will be used:

```
import socket

HOST = '19*.***.*.***'    # The remote host
PORT = 50007              # The same port as used by the server
s = socket.socket(socket.AF_INET, socket.SOCK_STREAM)
s.connect((HOST, PORT))
```

Port 50007 is used because nothing else is using it. Now the client starts the conversation, just as it appears at the beginning of this section:

```
s.send(b'Hi there!')
```

The **send**() function sends the message passed as a parameter. The string (as *bytes*) is transmitted to the server through the variable **s**, which represents the server. The client now waits for the confirmation string from the server, which should be "Hello. Nice to see you." The client calls:

```
data = s.recv(1024)
```

which waits for a response from the server. This response will be 1024-bytes long at most, and it will wait only for a short time, at which point it will give up and an error will be reported. When this client gets the response, it proceeds to send numbers to the server. They are converted into the *bytes* type before transmission. In this example it simply loops through 100 consecutive integers:

```
for i in range (0, 100):
    data = str(i).encode()
    s.send (data)
```

After sending to the server it waits for the answer. Actually that's a part of the receive function:

```
    data = s.recv(1024)
```

after 100 integers the loop ends and the connection is closed:

```
s.close()
```

The Server: is always listening. It creates a socket on a particular port so that the operating system knows something is possible there, but because the server cannot predict when a client will connect or what client it will be, it simply listens for a connection, by calling a function named **listen()**:

```
import socket
from random import *

HOST = ''    # A null string is correct here.
PORT = 50007
s = socket.socket(socket.AF_INET, socket.SOCK_STREAM)
s.bind ((HOST, PORT))
s.listen()
```

AF_INET and SOCK_STREAM are constants that tells the system which protocols are being used. These are the most common, but see the documentation for others. The **bind()** and the **listen()** functions are new. Associating this connection with a specific port is done using **bind()**. The tuple (HOST, PORT) says to connect this host to this port. The empty string for HOST implies *this* computer. The **listen()** call starts the server process, *this* program, accepting connections when asked. A process connecting on the port that was specified in *bind()* will now result in this process, the server, being notified. When a connection request occurs, the server must accept it before doing any input or output:

```
conn, addr = s.accept()
```

In the tuple (**conn, addr**) that is returned, **conn** represents the connection, like a file descriptor returned from **open()**, and is used to send and receive data; **addr** is the address of the sender, the client, and is a string. If the **addr** were printed:

```
print ("Connected to ", addr)
```

It would look like an IP address:

```
Connected to 423.141.12.911
```

Now the server can receive data across the connection, and does so by calling **recv()**:

```
data = conn.recv(1024)
print ("Server heard '", data, "'")
```

The parameter 1024 specifies the size of the buffer, or the maximum number of bytes that can be received in one call. The variable **data** is of type *bytes*, just as the parameter to **send()** was in the client. The client was the first to send, and it sent the message "Hi there!" That should be the value of data now, if it has been received properly. The response from the server should be "Hello, nice to see you.":

```
conn.send (b'Hello. Nice to see you.')
```

The same connection is used for sending and receiving.

Now the real data gets exchanged. The server will accept integers, sent as *bytes*. It will square them and transmit the answer back.

```
while True:
    data = conn.recv(1024)          # Read the incoming data
    if data:
        i = int(data)               # Convert it to integer
        print ("Received ", i)
        data = str(i*i).encode()    # Square it and
                                    # convert to bytes
        conn.send (data)            # Send to the client
```

The server can tell when the connection is closed by the client, but it is also polite to say "Goodbye" somehow, perhaps by sending a particular code. If the loop ever terminates, the server should close the connection:

```
    conn.close()
```

This is a pretty good example of a data exchange and a contract, because there are specified requirements for each side of this conversation which will result in success if done correctly and failure if messed up. Failure is sometimes indicated by an error message, often a *timeout* where the client or server was expecting something that never arrived. In other cases failure is not formally indicated at all; the program simply "hangs" there and does nothing. If at any time both processes are trying to receive data, then the program will fail.

Figure 9.2 shows the communication between the client and the server as a diagram. If the client and the server are at any time both trying to accept data from the connection, then the program will fail. In the diagram all data transfers can be seen as transmit-accept pairs between the two processes, and as read-write pairs within the server and write-read pairs within the client.

The FTP protocol can now be seen as a socket connection, wherein the client sends strings (commands) to the server, which parses them, carries out the request, and then sends an acknowledgment back.

```
# The client                    # The server
import socket                    import socket

# The remote host               HOST = '' # A null string is ok
HOST = '19*.***.*.***'                    here.
# The same port used by         PORT = 50007
the server                      s = socket.socket(socket.
PORT = 50007                        AF_INET, \
s = socket.socket(socket.           socket.SOCK_STREAM)
AF_INET,\                       s.bind ((HOST, PORT))
    socket.SOCK_STREAM)         s.listen()
s.connect((HOST, PORT))         conn, addr = s.accept()
s.send(b'Hi there!')            data = conn.recv(1024)
data = s.recv(1024)             print ("Server heard '", data, "'")
for i in range (0, 100):        conn.send (b'Hello. Nice
    data = str(i).encode()          to see you.')
    s.send (data)               while True:
    data = s.recv(1024)         # Read the incoming data
s.close()                           data = conn.recv(1024)
                                    if data:
                                # Convert it to integer
                                        i = int(data)
                                        print ("Received ", i)
                                # Square it and convert to bytes
                                        data = str(i*i).encode()
                                # Send to the client
                                        conn.send (data)
                                    conn.close()
```

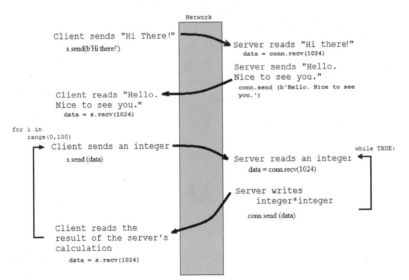

FIGURE 9.2 Typical communication between the client and the server processes

INDEX